amigurume

amigurume

MAKE CUTE CROCHET PEOPLE

Allison Hoffman

LARK

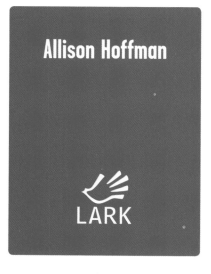

LARK

An Imprint of Sterling Publishing
387 Park Avenue South
New York, NY 10016

ISBN 978-1-4547-0397-6

Hoffman, Allison.
  AmiguruME / Allison Hoffman. -- First Edition.
     pages cm
  Includes index.
  ISBN 978-1-4547-0397-6
  1. Amigurumi--Patterns. 2. Soft toy making--Patterns. I. Title.
  TT829.H635 2013
  746.43'4043--dc23
                              2012040468

Distributed in Canada by Sterling Publishing
c/o Canadian Manda Group, 165 Dufferin Street
Toronto, Ontario, Canada M6K 3H6
Distributed in the United Kingdom by GMC Distribution Services
Castle Place, 166 High Street, Lewes, East Sussex, England BN7 1XU
Distributed in Australia by Capricorn Link (Australia) Pty. Ltd.
P.O. Box 704, Windsor, NSW 2756, Australia

For information about custom editions, special sales, and premium and
corporate purchases, please contact Sterling Special Sales at 800-805-5489
or specialsales@sterlingpublishing.com.

Email academic@larkbooks.com for information about desk and
examination copies. The complete policy can be found at larkcrafts.com.

Manufactured in China

2 4 6 8 10 9 7 5 3 1

larkcrafts.com

This isn't a standard crochet pattern book—it's more like a "choose your own ending"-style of crochet book. For each part of your doll, you'll mix and match following only the pattern (or occasionally patterns) you want from each section. Each choice you make will come together in a one-of-a-kind doll!

HAIR
Mohawks to mustaches: the long and short of it

MAKING FACES AND HEADS
Many differents kinds to choose from

ACCESSORIES
Make all the difference

UPPER BODY
From a basic tee to separate outerwear

LOWER BODY
Shorts, pants, and skirts

FEET AND SHOES
From flip-flops to boots

★ These patterns are for the garment only. You'll need to pick one of the other *upper body patterns* to pair with them.

★ ★ These patterns are for the garment only. You'll need to pick one of the other *lower body patterns* (like tights or bare legs and underwear) to pair with them.

INTRODUCTION

One day I was looking at crafts online when I came across the word *amigurumi*. I'd seen it a few times before but had no idea what the word meant or what it was. A quick search and I found out amigurumi literally translated in Japanese means "knitted stuffed toy."

A year prior I'd learned basic knitting stitches and made a funny-looking scarf. It took a long time. I was using cheap yarn and huge metal needles, and I didn't have any urge to start another project after I finished it. I hung up that scarf in my closet and proudly proclaimed, "Well, I know how to knit! Moving on..."

Upon further investigation, I found out that traditional amigurumi was, in fact, crocheted, not knitted. I hate to say it, but I had a somewhat negative opinion of knitting's sister-craft. Frilly toilet seat covers and bleach bottle cozies in garish colors of scratchy yarn came to mind. The crochet I was familiar with looked nothing like these sweet little softies with diminutive smiles and wide-set eyes. The tiny toys I was finding online looked so difficult to make, but I wanted to do it!

I plunged in headfirst. Some people start out crocheting dishcloths or making granny squares, but I wasn't really interested in either. Don't get me wrong: I've since learned to crochet those beautiful granny squares with the best of them and can appreciate the value of a handmade dishcloth. But when I was starting out, I just had to make toys! I sought out several basic crochet videos online and bought a cheap hook and ball of yarn. I definitely missed a step on my first few attempts. Although I wasn't exactly clear on what I was doing wrong, I decided to just keep going. Nothing was unraveling, so I figured I was onto something. Crocheting in a circle, around and around and around, I soon had the basic shape of a little bear. There were lots of holes--huge, gaping holes, in fact--and he was very lopsided. None of his limbs were the same size. Stuffing poked out all over. I pushed on, gave him a couple of eyes and embroidered him a wee mouth and nose. I was so proud of myself! I made amigurumi! He wasn't anywhere near perfect, but if you squinted and held him at arms' distance he was actually pretty cute.

I couldn't stop there. Watching crochet videos online, I finally got my stitches right and tried several basic patterns. I loved playing with the shaping to make the toys just how I envisioned them. From there, it snowballed. Each of my kids wanted their own. My little boys had an endless stream of ideas for toys I could make that looked like their favorite superheroes, movie stars, and video-game characters. I started writing down patterns, opened up shop on Ravelry.com, and started CraftyisCool.com. I began cranking out patterns for all sorts of designs, focusing on pop culture and trying to make each doll totally unique.

Almost immediately, I had several requests for custom dolls. One customer wanted a doll that looked like her husband when he had proposed to her years before. Another requested a doll that looked like her coworker. It was a Christmas present for the person who had everything. I started keeping a log of pattern alterations and ideas to expand upon.

Besides writing patterns and making dolls for custom orders, I started making dolls of some people I really loved, just for fun. It started with Conan O'Brien. My husband and I loved watching him on his late-night talk show and when he took over the *The Tonight Show*, we never missed an episode. We felt jilted right along with Conan and his legions of fans when he was forced out and lost his job. There was a group uprising, and I did my small part (at my husband's urging) and made a Conan doll. The "I'm With Coco" group on Facebook gave one away in a contest online and the doll went viral. Bloggers like Perez Hilton and entertainment news sites like Entertainment Weekly featured the doll. When I sent Conan a giant stuffed crocheted blimp, he showcased it on his blog and Twitter account, and later he used it as a prop on his show. My husband and I traveled to a taping of his new show in Los Angeles, and he invited me to come backstage, where I finally got to meet him and give him his own little Conan doll.

After such a great experience with Conan, I wanted to spread the love! I heard Paul "Pee-wee Herman" Reubens was going to be in town. He was one of my childhood idols and is one of my favorite people in the world. I knew I just had to make a Pee-wee doll. Word got back to Pee-wee's people, and I was invited by Mr. Reubens to a personal appearance and gave him his doll in person.

I made a Martha Stewart doll, because how could I not craft a craft queen? The Martha Stewart doll I made caught Martha's attention, and she invited me to New York, where I personally gave her the doll and told her about my work and inspiration on her show.

Are you noticing a theme here? Dolls that look like people, famous or just family, are super fun to make (and give as gifts)! Just as I found inspiration in my love of pop culture and kitsch, your first step is answering the question: Who are you trying to make as a doll? What are their distinguishing features or signature items of clothing? When you start reading through these pages, I hope you have some fun envisioning what you want your doll to look like. Each part of your creation will be up to you.

If you just bought your first crochet hook and need to learn the basics, you'll want to start on page 10. You'll learn how to choose tools, what yarns work best for amigurumi, and how to execute the most common crochet stitches. You'll probably be relieved to know that only the most basic stitches are required! As with most crochet projects, with a few techniques, you will be able to crochet pretty much anything you want.

If you have a grasp of all the basic stitches, you can skip ahead to page 32 and start a doll. From there, each section of the book deals with a part of the doll. There's the head, where you can choose from different shapes. Then you'll continue down the body, choosing what you want your doll's clothing to look like. Dress him up in a suit and tie or give her a casual sundress and flip-flops! Next you'll create your doll's hairstyle. Will he have a mohawk or a ponytail? The last step will be to create tiny accessories to make your doll come to life. Does she play the guitar? Is he wearing a hat? Add elements that make your doll an individual!

I hope you enjoy using these designs to make a doll that's all your own. Let your imagination be your guide. You may be surprised at how the tiniest details give your doll a unique personality. Whether you're making a gift or a doll that looks just like you (or both!), I hope you're already feeling inspired to create your very own "amiguruME."

GETTING STARTED

MATERIALS

One of the funnest parts of making amigurumi dolls (besides designing them and giving them away) is buying the materials that will become your creation. Of course, you'll need yarn, but maybe you haven't thought of all the other materials you get to pick out. Each choice will add more customization, more personality, and more embellishment to the end product. Use your imagination. Instead of seeing balls of yarn on the craft-store shelf, envision outfits, hair, and accessories!

Yarn

There are literally thousands of options when it's time to choose your yarn. Everyone has an opinion. Some people won't touch acrylic yarn with a ten-foot pole. Some crafters are allergic to wool. Cotton can be rough and hard to work with for some, but its natural quality appeals to others.

For constructing the main bodies and heads of amigurumi, I always recommend worsted-weight yarn. It is the most common weight of yarn and comes in a plethora of colors and fibers. It is thick enough

to be structured when crocheted tightly, while still remaining soft. For specific types of yarn I recommend, check out page 12.

What if you find the perfect color yarn and it's not the right weight? If it's too fine, try holding two strands together. The combined strands should prove a suitable substitution and perform like a worsted weight.

Stuffing

What makes these dolls so squeezably soft and fun to hold? They are packed with stuffing! It's obvious that you'll need to pick out a stuffing you like to work with, because you'll be working with it quite a bit. There are many options, including 100% polyester (which is what I like to use most of the time), wool roving (a more expensive but all-natural choice), bamboo, spun corn fibers, and even leftover yarn scraps or cotton balls! Be warned: Some stuffings may clump easily and make your doll misshapen over time. Be careful trying anything you haven't used before, especially lumpier options like leftover yarn or cotton balls.

Safety Eyes

I get lots of questions regarding dolls' eyes. They aren't available everywhere, and some people (including yours truly) have resorted at times to simply sewing on rounded buttons for eyes. But this doesn't always work, and the buttons usually come loose and look strangely sad and droopy over time.

Some craft stores carry plastic safety eyes in their doll-making sections. When you do find them, they are often in limited supply and very limited in variety. So I usually order doll eyes online. There are many great sellers that specialize in this kind of thing, and they carry eyes in so many colors and sizes it will make your head spin (see Resources, page 124). As you might notice, I usually go for a more cartoonish look and stick with basic black. It never goes out of style!

The safety eyes have a shaft that sticks through the fabric and a washer that snaps onto the shaft from inside. They must be inserted before closing up and stuffing your doll's head, and each head pattern gives instructions on placement and at which point they should be used.

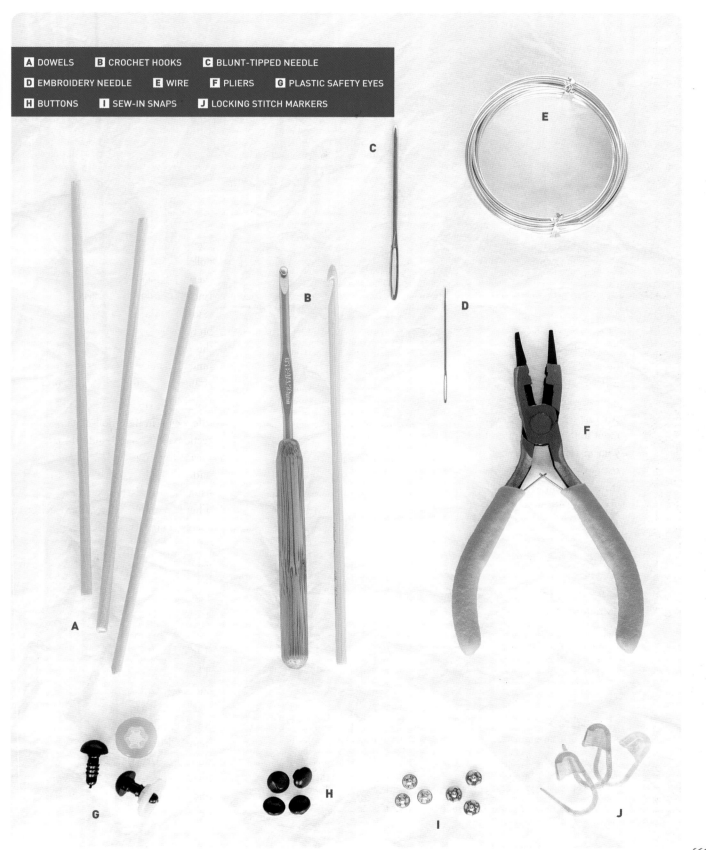

A DOWELS   B CROCHET HOOKS   C BLUNT-TIPPED NEEDLE
D EMBROIDERY NEEDLE   E WIRE   F PLIERS   G PLASTIC SAFETY EYES
H BUTTONS   I SEW-IN SNAPS   J LOCKING STITCH MARKERS

Choosing Yarn

Yarn for Skin Tones

One of the questions I get most frequently is about choosing yarn for the doll's skin tone. In short, a light peach is perfect for a Caucasian doll. I've found that even a pale off-white can be a great choice for a doll's main color. After all, once you add hair, clothing, and a little blush to the cheeks, the doll won't look so pale. Darker skin tones are easily achieved by using anything from tans to dark browns. Most yarn companies produce lots of choices for this range of colors.

In order from lighter skin tone to darker, here's a list of several of my favorite, easy-to-find, worsted-weight yarns to use for a doll's main skin color:

■ Caron Simply Soft #9737 Light Country Peach

■ Cascade 220 #9493 Salmon

■ Lion Brand Martha Stewart Crafts Extra Soft Wool Blend #599 Buttermilk

■ Lion Brand Vanna's Choice #123 Beige

■ Caron Simply Soft #9703 Bone

■ Caron Simply Soft #0006 Sand

■ Cascade 220 #9499 Sand

■ Red Heart Soft #9388 Wheat

■ Cascade 220 Wool #9498 Bark

■ Red Heart Soft #1882 Toast

■ Bernat Sheep(ish) by Vickie Howell #00010 Camel(ish)

■ Lion Brand Vanna's Choice #124 Toffee

■ Lion Brand Martha Stewart Crafts Extra Soft Wool Blend #526 Sable

■ Cascade 220 Wool #9497 Brown Bear

■ Lion Brand Vanna's Choice #126 Chocolate

Most of the yarns listed above are acrylic. The exceptions are wools and wool blends. There are many substitutions for these yarns, but the list represents a good base range of which colors to look for. There are many more not listed here. You may find great choices at your local yarn store if you're looking with "amiguruME eyes."

Yarn for Clothing

The first thing you will look at when you're choosing the yarn for your doll's clothing is color. While it's true that color is very important, you should also make sure you are choosing the right weight of yarn. A simple rule to follow is that if the clothing is removable, you should crochet it out of sport-weight yarn. Why sport weight? I have found that clothing crocheted out of worsted-weight yarn tends to come out stiff without much drape. Sport-weight yarn will make the clothing softer and more flexible, and it will look more like fabric. There can be exceptions, of course. If you just can't find the right color in sport-weight yarn, feel free to substitute worsted weight. Some very soft worsted-weight yarns will work just fine.

The same is not true for clothes that are part of the doll's body. When you are crocheting a doll with attached clothing (like pants and shirts), make sure you choose worsted-weight. A lighter weight yarn will create a fabric with too many holes, and then you'll have stuffing showing or poking through—something you definitely don't want. The worsted-weight yarn will give stability and a slight stiffness that works well for the main body of your doll. And if you don't remember this later, that's okay. Each pattern in the book will suggest a yarn weight. If you're unable to find the yarn you need in a worsted-weight, feel free to substitute with a lighter weight yarn, holding two (or more, if necessary) strands together. The combined strands provide a gauge heavy enough to give your doll structure.

Yarn for Hair

This is where the fun begins! There are as many textures of yarn as there are textures of human hair. From boucle to eyelash, different kinds of yarn will produce different kinds of hair. When you choose the yarn for your doll's hair, you get to check out the yarns you might never use otherwise in amigurumi:

Will your doll have an Afro?
Use a boucle yarn.

Want your doll's hair to be pin-straight?
Look for a sport weight.

Should your doll sport a brightly colored mohawk?
Take a look at the fun colors of eyelash yarn available.

We'll discuss even more possibilities for hair later (page 90), and you'll see how your yarn choice will make all the difference.

If you're making a doll for a young child, you may want to glue or sew on felt circles for the eyes instead. When my kids were toddlers, they always found a way to pop those little eyes out of their washers and off the doll's face! Luckily, none were eaten, but they were replaced with kid-friendly felt appliqués just in case.

Felt

From time to time you may need to use felt on your amigurumi. If you'd like to add a pocket square to your doll's jacket, embellish your doll's T-shirt with a felt appliqué, or substitute soft and safe felt eyes for the plastic ones, you're going to want to find a strong felt fabric. Most felt you'll find at craft stores is polyester and fine to use, but if your doll will be played with you will want to choose carefully. Look through the felt and choose the thickest, sturdiest pieces you can find. Even in the same color, the options may vary widely. If you have trouble finding suitable polyester-blend felt or if you'd like to use a natural fiber, look for a wool or wool blend. Again, there are lots of places online to buy small quantities of felt at great prices in every color of the rainbow.

Embroidery Floss

You'll need a small stash of embroidery floss, mainly in black and red, for embroidering details on your amigurumi. I use the full six strands to embroider facial features like smiles, eyebrows, eyelashes, and freckles.

Buttons and Snaps

I always have a good supply of tiny buttons and metal snap fasteners to use on my dolls' clothes. There are lots of different sizes available in the sewing department of any craft store. I use the buttons on the outside where they will be seen, and hide the functional snaps on the insides of jackets and sweaters so that the dolls can be dressed and undressed.

Other Embellishments

As far as embellishing your amigurumi goes, the sky is the limit. If you want to go crazy with your doll's clothing, there are as many beads, sequins, ribbons, and trims as you could ask for. Rickrack makes an adorable trim on a skirt, and adding a few beads on a string of yarn makes a unique bracelet. Use your imagination!

TOOLS

Besides the glorious yarn and other great materials you get to pick out when you start making these dolls, you're going to need a few basic tools. Putting together a good amigurumi tool kit is just as important as picking out the right yarn!

Hooks

The crochet hook is your new best friend. If you don't pick a hook you like working with, you'll get cramped hands—and after about 10 minutes you'll be ready to throw in the towel. If possible, go to your local yarn store and try out a few. Decide what you like or don't like about each one. There are plastic, aluminum, wood, and steel hooks. My favorite hooks are those with ergonomic handles. The larger grip keeps your hand from getting stressed, and the shaft and tip of the hooks are shaped perfectly for the tight gauge you'll be working in for amigurumi. They cost a few dollars more than other hooks, but there is no comparison in my opinion. When I have to use a standard hook in a size that I don't have an ergonomic hook for, my hand is stiff afterward for hours.

Each pattern will instruct you on which size hook you'll need, and don't be surprised to see that the hooks are a little smaller than you'd use for, say, an afghan. Amigurumi needs to be crocheted very tightly so that there aren't little holes all over the fabric, which will allow stuffing to poke through.

Needles

You're going to need a couple of different needles for your amigurumi. Yarn needles are large, blunt-tipped needles with large eyes made for sewing with yarn. When you assemble your amigurumi, you'll use a yarn needle to sew the parts together. There are amazing yarn needles with bent tips that allow you to sew into surfaces with ease. You will also need an embroidery needle for embroidering details onto your doll.

Scissors

It's very important to have a good pair of pointed-end sharp scissors in your tool kit. You'll mainly be using them for snipping yarn ends, but if you plan on using them to cut felt shapes you'll want them to be relatively small.

Other Items

After the three most important tools, you should make sure you have a few other items. I always have a bottle of high-quality craft glue. I use it for gluing small bits of felt when sewing the felt on isn't practical. For stuffing the dolls, I use a stuffing tool (a long wooden stick with a pointed end, much like a knitting needle). If you don't have a stuffing tool, you can use a knitting needle, chopstick, wooden dowel, or even the end of your crochet hook. Locking stitch markers are also important to have on hand. When you reach a point in your work in which you need to stuff or add eyes, you will be instructed to insert a stitch marker to hold your place. Stitch markers can also be inserted into the loop on your hook when you are starting a new round.

Download the guitar pattern seen here at: LarkCrafts.com/bonus

The amigurumi in this book is crocheted in spiral rounds, which will help you keep track and count stitches and rounds. Each time you come back around to the stitch marker, move it up to the loop on your hook to begin the next round. A measuring tape is helpful for measuring pattern elements as you go.

Special Tools

When I first started making amigurumi dolls, I had to overcome the whole "huge heavy head on a skinny body" problem. There was no way the head was going to stand up without some support, so I improvised. I used to break a chopstick in half and stick it into the head, half into the body through the neck, and then sew the pieces together. Since then I've found wooden dowel rods at the craft store that work perfectly. I still have to break them in half, but they are smooth and the perfect size for the job.

I like to make my amigurumi poseable. This is another one of those things that you should NOT do if the doll is going to be for a child. Basically, heavy-gauge (16 to 19) wire is inserted into an arm, through the body, and out the other side. The wire is then inserted into the other arm. The wire ends are bent with needle-nose pliers, another optional tool for your growing amigurumi tool kit.

KEEPING IT TOGETHER

When you've acquired all of your tools, keep them together in a toolbox or zippered pouch that you can easily fit into your project bag. I use a custom-made fabric roll meant for crayons to store my crochet hooks and keep the rest of my tools in a sectioned plastic toolbox with a handle.

HOW TO CROCHET

Now it's time to familiarize yourself with all of the basic skills you'll need to create your first (or your fiftieth) amigurumi. If you already know how to crochet, skim through the crochet information and jump right into the next chapter, though you might want to glance at some of the stuffing and assembly techniques on page 30. If crocheting is new to you, let's get started!

GET A GRIP

Pencil grip

Overhand grip

People hold their crochet hooks in many different ways. The two basic grips are the pencil grip and the overhand grip. I usually tell people to try the pencil grip first, because it is more common, but each person has to do what feels comfortable.

There are lots of variations. Even though I always grip mine like a pencil, I rarely see anyone that holds it exactly the same.

Once you figure out the grip that works for you, start practicing the basic stitches for amigurumi below.

Start with the chain stitch to get a feeling of how crochet works. Each stitch includes the abbreviation most commonly used in U.S. crochet patterns in parentheses ().

HANDLING YARN

You've got your hook in one hand and your yarn in the other. When you start crocheting, you'll be holding your work and yarn in the same hand. You'll have to find what is comfortable for you. Usually the thumb grips the work and the yarn is wrapped around the index finger or the pinky. Wrapping the yarn around your fingers gives it tension so that it will create a sturdy, even fabric.

As you work crochet stitches, keep in mind that every time you move the yarn around the hook, a step that's referred to as a "yarn over" or "yo," you will wrap the yarn from the back to the front.

CHAIN STITCH (ch)

A

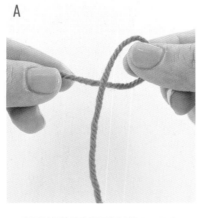

B

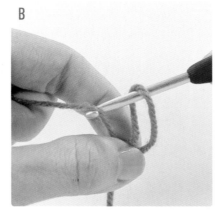

C

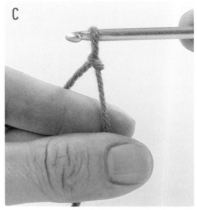

D

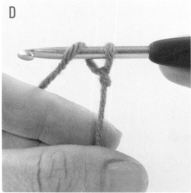

E

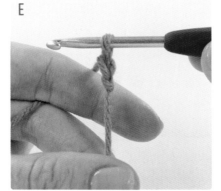

F

The chain stitch is used as a foundation stitch, especially when crocheting something flat in rows. It is also used at the end of rows for turning.

1 To make a chain stitch, begin with a slip knot on your hook. This knot does not count as a stitch, but is simply holding the yarn on your hook for you to do the first stitch. (A, B, C)

2 Holding your hook in one hand and the yarn coming from the ball in the other hand, bring the yarn over the hook (yarn over). It will look like there are two loops of yarn lying over the top of your hook. (D)

3 "Catch" the yarn that you just wrapped and pull it through the first loop on your hook. One loop will remain on your hook and you've just completed one chain stitch! (E) Repeat steps 2 and 3 for as many chains as the pattern calls for. (F)

Each stitch will be a "v" shape. Keep that in mind as you start counting your stitches. The slip knot we started with will not look like a "v" and will not be counted as a stitch. The chain will have a "v" on the front and a little bump on the back. When you start crocheting into a chain, your goal will be to insert your hook between the "v" on top and the bump on the back. This is challenging, even for experienced crocheters, and many people (ahem!) cheat a little and insert the hook into the middle of the "v" for that first row of stitches, or even into the back bar or bump of the chain. It leaves a nice lower edge. Try it several ways and see what is most comfortable for you.

SLIP STITCH (sl st)

The slip stitch is mainly used to move around your work without adding much height to your crocheted piece. It can also be used to join rounds in circular crochet. Because we will be using the Adjustable Ring method for crocheting in the round, which you'll learn next, the slip stitch will be used mainly for fastening off work.

1 Insert the hook into the next stitch. Pull up a loop.

2 Pull the loop all the way through the loop on your hook. One slip stitch has been made.

SURFACE SLIP STITCH

Surface slip stitches are sometimes used for surface embellishment. Work a round of slip stitch in a different color for a belt. Then work the next round into the same single crochets "behind" the slip stitches, and continue on your way. Work "surface slip stitch" over the surface of a finished piece to draw lines, squiggles, and so on.

SINGLE CROCHET (sc)

G

H

I

J

Let's go over the stitch you'll need for all of the patterns in this book. It's pretty much the easiest stitch in crochet, and the good news is that if you can learn this stitch, you'll have no trouble mastering any other crochet stitch, because all of the others are basically variations on this one. Almost all amigurumi is done in single crochet. It produces a tight, stiff fabric that is excellent for stuffed animals and toys. The instructions below address crocheting into stitches. Of course, when you start, you will crochet into a chain (for rows in flat projects) or a ring (for rounds). Try out a few rows of single crochet just to get a feel for it. You'll be an expert in no time.

1 Insert your hook into the front of the fabric (or chain), under both loops of the stitch (or chain), (G) and pull a loop through to the front. Two loops are on your hook. (H)

2 Wrap the working yarn around your hook. There are three loops on your hook. (I) Pull the last loop through the first two loops. Only one loop remains on the hook. This is one single crochet stitch. (J)

ADJUSTABLE RING METHOD

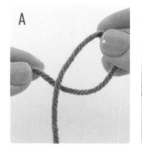

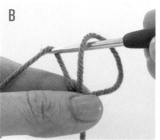

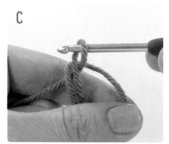

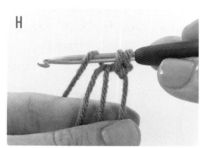

Making an adjustable ring only requires a few extra steps and will give your in-the-round projects a smooth start. There are alternative ways to start crocheting in the round, but other methods leave tiny holes. The chain stitch you just learned will be used only once, in the very beginning, but is a key element.

1 Begin by making a small ring or loop with the yarn, crossing the end of the yarn over the front of the working yarn, leaving a 6"/15cm tail. This ring will be closed in the last step. **(A)**

2 Hold where both strands of yarn overlap along the ring, keeping the working yarn behind the ring. Moving from front to back, insert your crochet hook into the ring **(B)** and pull up a loop from the working yarn. **(C)** Make one chain stitch (ch) by yarning over from back to front and pulling through the loop on your hook. There will be one loop on your hook. **(D, E)**

3 Insert your crochet hook back into the ring. **(F)** Pull a loop of working yarn through the center of the ring. **(G)**

4 Now there are two loops on your crochet hook. Yarn over and pull through both loops, completing a single crochet stitch (sc). **(H, I)**

Continue crocheting around both the tail and the ring, repeating steps 3 and 4, until you have the desired number of single crochet stitches. **(J)** When you do, gently pull on the yarn tail to close up the ring. The ring of stitches you have just created will be the base for all of the rest of your stitches and counts as the first round.

HALF DOUBLE CROCHET (hdc)

K

L

M

N

O

Half double crochet stitches are exactly what they imply. They are half of a double crochet stitch, which you'll learn next. They are a little taller than a single crochet.

1 Before inserting your hook under the stitch, yarn over. (K) Continue on as if you were going to make a single crochet. Insert your hook under the "v" of the next stitch (L) and pull up a loop. Now you will have three loops on your hook. (M)

2 Wrap the working yarn around your hook. There are four loops on your hook. (N) Pull the last loop through the first three loops. Only one loop remains on the hook. This completes one half double crochet stitch. (O)

DOUBLE CROCHET (dc)

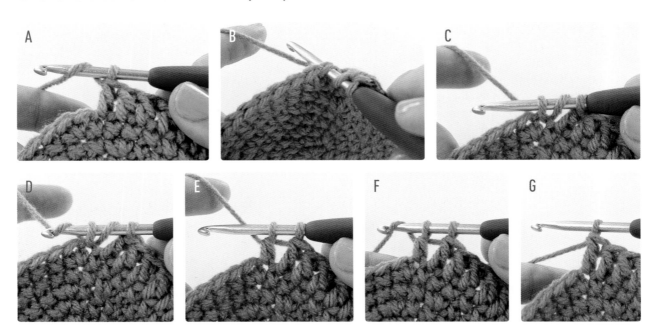

A double crochet stitch is twice as tall as a single crochet stitch.

1 Wrap the yarn around the hook (yarn over) **(A)** and insert your hook into the next stitch. **(B)** Pull up a loop. Three loops will be on your hook. **(C)**

2 Yarn over **(D)** and pull the yarn through the first two loops on the hook. **(E)** Two loops will be on the hook.

3 Yarn over again **(F)** and pull the yarn through the last two loops on the hook. There will be one loop on the hook. One double crochet stitch has been made. **(G)**

BOBBLE STITCH

Now that you've learned the double crochet stitch, you will use that new skill to make a bobble. The bobble is used in my amigurumi patterns for noses, thumbs, and toes. Every bobble stitch used in the book will have a specific number next to it in the pattern notes, signifying how many double crochets are used. You will see this in patterns written like this: bobble [5 dc].

1 Yarn over (H) and insert the hook into the next stitch. (I) Pull up a loop. (J) Three loops will be on the hook.

2 Yarn over (K) and pull through just two loops. Two loops remain on your hook. (L)

3 Repeat steps 1 and 2 into the same stitch (M) until you've made the required number of double crochets as indicated in []. Each time step 2 is completed, there will be one more loop on your hook. When you've made the required number of double crochets, the number of loops on your hook will be one more than the number of double crochets you made. For example, if the pattern calls for bobble [5 dc], you will have six loops on your hook. (N)

4 Yarn over (O) and pull through all the loops on your hook. One loop remains on your hook and you've made one bobble stitch. (P)

When you crochet into the next stitch, the bobble stitch you just made will puff out. (Q) You may need to help the bobble puff out to the right side of the fabric by gently pushing it to the outside.

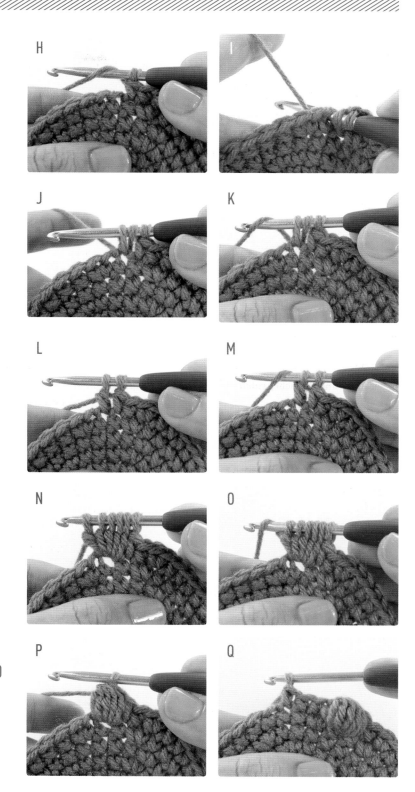

INCREASING

Increasing in crochet is very simple. You will crochet two stitches into one stitch. Increases in rounds are spaced evenly, as written in each pattern. A note about increasing in rounds: by staggering the increases, the finished piece will have a rounder shape. For example, crocheting a few stitches before beginning an increase repeat will make the increase blend in easily, while stacking the increases, or increasing in the same spot in each round, is more noticeable.

DECREASING

To decrease, you have several options.

Single Crochet Two Together (Sc2tog)

You may single crochet two stitches together (sc2tog) by inserting your hook into the next stitch (A), pulling up a loop (B), inserting into the next stitch (C) and pulling up another loop, (D) and then yarning over (E) and pulling the loop through all the loops on your hook. One loop remains and you have created one sc2tog decrease. (F) This is the traditional method used but may leave tiny gaps before and after the stitch. When working in rows, as in the dolls' removable clothing, I like to use the sc2tog decrease.

DECREASING

Invisible Decrease (Invdec)

Another method of decreasing is the invisible decrease. This creates a less noticeable stitch and is a favorite of amigurumi lovers. Moving your hook from the front to the back of each stitch, insert your hook into the front loop only of the next two stitches (G) and pull a loop up through both (H). Two loops are on your hook. Yarn over (I) and pull through both loops. One loop remains on your hook and you have made one invdec. (J)

Double Crochet Two Together (Dc2tog)

Decrease with a double crochet by yarning over, (A) inserting your hook into the next stitch (B) and pulling up a loop, (C) yarning over (D), drawing through two loops (E), yarning over (F) and inserting the hook into the next stitch (G) and pulling up a loop (H), yarning over (I) and drawing through two loops (J), and finally yarning over (K) and drawing through all three loops on your hook.(L) You are essentially completing half of a double crochet twice, before crocheting them together for the final step in the stitch.

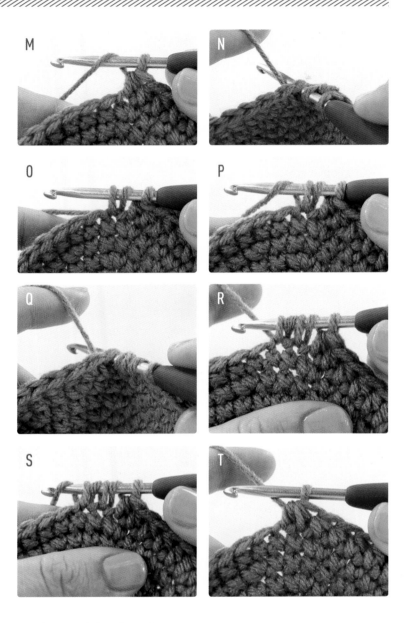

Half Double Crochet Two Together (Hdc2tog)

Some patterns will call for a decrease while you are working in half double crochet stitches. In this case you will use the hdc2tog decrease. Yarn over, (M) insert your hook into the next stitch, (N) yarn over and pull up a loop, (O) and repeat into the next stitch. (P, Q) Five loops will remain on your hook. (R) Yarn over one last time (S) and pull through all loops on your hook, combining the two stitches and decreasing. (T)

CROCHETING INTO BACK LOOPS ONLY (BLO) OR FRONT LOOPS ONLY (FLO)

In most instances, each stitch is crocheted under both loops of the stitch. Sometimes it's necessary to crochet only into one loop of the stitch. This creates a little ridge on the front or back of the work, depending on which loop you crochet into, and makes a stretchier and somewhat thinner fabric. When a pattern calls for crocheting into the back loops only, or BLO, you will insert your hook into the middle of the "v" of the stitch, under only the back of the stitch. **(A)** If the pattern tells you to crochet into the front loops only, or FLO, you will insert your hook into the front of the stitch, under only the front loop, and out through the middle of the "v." **(B)**

CHANGING COLOR

There will come a time when you're crocheting that you either want to change colors or run out of yarn and need to add yarn from a new ball. It is quite simple to perform a quick change without making a single knot.

1 Work the last stitch before the change until the last step of the stitch, just before your last yarn over. (C)

2 Instead of finishing the stitch with the old yarn, drop it to the back and pull a loop of the new yarn through the remaining loops on the hook. (D) Continue to the next stitch with the new yarn. (E, F)

To secure the two ends, continue crocheting, laying the yarn tails on top of the stitches and crocheting over them several times. Clip them with several inches of length left over. After finishing the piece you are working on, you can weave in the ends with a yarn needle.

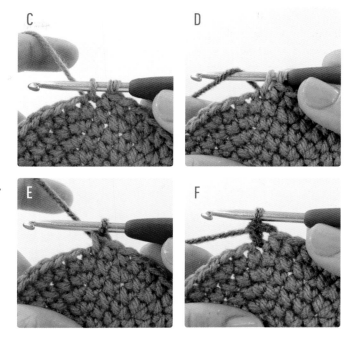

FASTENING OFF

So you've finished crocheting your masterpiece (or just a piece of it) and it's time to fasten things off.

Simply finish your last stitch, cut the yarn about 6"/15cm away from the stitch, and hook the strand, pulling it all the way through the loop on your hook.

When working in the round, after completing your final stitch, insert your hook into the next stitch (G), hook the strand (H), and pull it all the way up through the loop on your hook. (I, J) This is a slip stitch (sl st) and makes a smooth edge finish.

Finish by weaving in the yarn tail with a yarn needle. For stuffed toys, the end can be hidden inside the toy. Insert the needle into the toy all the way through to the other side, pulling tightly. Clip the yarn tail close to the surface, and let go, and the yarn tail will retract, hiding itself inside.

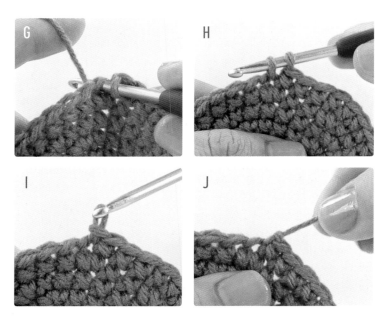

Surface Crochet

By crocheting on the surface of your work, you can add an element of design with slip stitches or create dimension with raised single-crochet stitches.

Surface Slip Stitch (Surface sl st)

This stitch is created by holding the working yarn under your work, inserting the hook where you want the first stitch, and pulling up a loop to the surface. Insert your hook back through the front of the fabric, a short distance from the previous insertion, pull up a loop, and pull it through the loop on your hook. Continue this process to create a series of interlocking slip stitches on the surface of the fabric. To finish, cut the yarn at the back and pull it through to the front, fastening off the last slip stitch, and weave in the ends.

Surface Single Crochet (Surface sc)

Here, single crochet stitches are worked horizontally on the surface of stitches. With a slip knot on your hook, insert the hook into the space before a crochet stitch, guide the hook around the back of the stitch and into the space on the other side of the stitch, bringing the hook back to the surface, then yarn over, pull up a loop through to where you first inserted your hook (two loops on hook), yarn over again, and pull through both loops on the hook. Continue this process for the required number of stitches, fasten off, and weave in the ends as directed in the pattern.

SPECIAL AMIGURUMI TECHNIQUES

There are several non-crochet techniques you'll need to learn that are unique to making amigurumi.

Stuff It

In the Materials section we discussed the all-important stuffing that goes into your doll. Once you've decided what you'll be stuffing into your doll, you should learn exactly how to stuff it. Forget what you've always heard about "less is more." The opposite is true. More is more! Because of the nature of the fluffy fiberfill, over time it will compress and any space you've left inside your doll will lose its shape. Amigurumi should be filled with as much stuffing as you can fit in as long as you are not stretching the fabric so that the stuffing is showing through the holes. If you think you've fit in as much stuffing as you can, try a little more. You may be surprised at how quickly you'll go through a big, 20-ounce (560g) bag of stuffing!

The smallest pieces you'll be stuffing are your doll's arms. If you wait until the end, you may have a tight squeeze. If you want to avoid this, stuff a little as you go. If you don't have that kind of patience and you want to get it all crocheted at once and worry about stuffing later (like me!), you'll want to stuff those tiny arms with a knitting needle, a chopstick, or maybe even the end of your crochet hook. Use tiny bits at a time or it will bunch up beyond

repair. Then you'll be trying to figure out how to pull those big, wadded-up pieces of stuffing out without ruining your work! Can you tell I am writing from experience?

Construct It

When you've crocheted the pieces of your doll, stuffed them, and you're ready to stick them together, what's next? Get out that yarn needle we talked about. You're going to start sewing—probably everyone's least favorite part of making amigurumi.

Some people like to use pins to hold the pieces together, then sew the body parts together. Many times the stitches will line right up and you can sew stitch to stitch, creating a seamless join. Most of the time, however, you're going to need to sew as discreetly as possible, up through one piece, out, back down through the other piece, out, and so on. Try not to split the yarn by sewing between stitches instead of through them. When you're finished, you can pull the yarn tightly, knot it close to the surface, let it retract back inside, and then weave the yarn back out through another spot. This will hide the knot inside and redirect the tail from coming out in the same spot.

Heavy Heads

Because my amigurumi are so top-heavy, I use a special trick to keep them from always looking down at the floor. In the Tools section (page 16), I mentioned buying narrow wooden dowels to use for holding heads up. Dowels are a very simple and effective way to give your amigurumi great posture.

Start by breaking the dowel into a piece that is about 5"/12.5cm long for an adult male- or female-sized doll, and 4"/10cm long for a child-proportioned doll. After stuffing the head firmly, insert one end into the base of the head a few rows behind the last row of stitches. After crocheting and stuffing the body piece of your amigurumi, insert the other end into the body. Use the yarn tail from the body to sew the pieces together, making sure they line up correctly and the dowel remains straight and aligned. Finish by knotting the tail close to the surface and threading it back inside the body, and then out, snipping it close to the surface.

Embroidery How-To

When you're finished crocheting your amigurumi, you'll want to add some embroidery for facial features, clothing embellishments, and other details. A few stitches are all you need for some interesting and effective details.

Straight Stitch

For simple eyelashes or other disconnected stitches, use a straight stitch of any length.

Stem Stitch

For bolder outline stitches, a stem or an outline stitch is appropriate. Working from left to right, make a small stitch. Keep the thread always on the same side of the needle and bring the needle up where the last stitch went in, following where you want a line, curved or straight.

Back Stitch

For a thin outline, use a back stitch. The stitches are small and even. Working from right to left, make a short stitch. Pull the needle back up a stitch ahead, and then insert it back down at the beginning of the first stitch. Continue working, connecting stitches backward.

French Knot

A French knot is a great stitch for making freckles, beauty marks, or tiny polka dots and flowers. Pull the needle up, wrap thread around the needle two or three times, and insert the needle close to where it came out. Tighten the thread with your other hand, forming a knot, while pulling the thread through to the back.

MAKING FACES AND HEADS

Let's face it. You can practice making a doll all day long, but if you don't capture your subject's face, it will be just another doll. If you face this problem head on, your dolls will be headed in the right direction. Okay, sorry, that was corny, but truthfully, if you make the right head shape, get the smile and mouth just so, position the eyes accurately, and get those freckles in the perfect spot, everyone who sees your doll should be able to recognize who you made.

Because nobody has a perfectly round head, you don't have to strive for perfection when you crochet this part of the doll. A little unevenness will give it a human quality! Shaping techniques will also give your doll character. Look at the options and choose the one that you feel will best suit your creation.

Structurally, the faces work like this: A nose is crocheted in as you go for all the designs, and the last few rows form a chin. Eyes are inserted toward the end, as well as plenty of stuffing, before closing off the finished head. As with all the main body parts in the book, keep the stitches tight so the finished fabric won't have holes for the stuffing to poke through.

There are two patterns for male heads, two patterns for female heads, and two patterns for children's heads. While it may be tempting to jump ahead and add hair after you've completed the doll's head, I've found that crocheting the rest of the body and attaching it to the head is much easier without the hair getting in the way. After the head is attached to the body, you'll also have a better perspective on hair position, length, and proportion.

LONG AND NARROW MALE HEAD

Why the long face? Actually, this face isn't overly long. It's just a bit narrower and taller than the other option for your guy dolls.

Materials and Tools

- WORSTED-WEIGHT YARN IN THE FLESH COLOR OF YOUR CHOICE (A) (REFER TO PAGE 12 FOR A LIST OF RECOMMENDED YARNS) **(4)**
- CROCHET HOOK: 3.5MM (SIZE E-4 U.S.)
- STITCH MARKER
- YARN NEEDLE
- BLACK 10MM SAFETY EYES
- POLYESTER FIBERFILL STUFFING

Stitches and Techniques Used

- ADJUSTABLE RING, PAGE 20
- CHAIN (CH), PAGE 18
- SINGLE CROCHET (SC), PAGE 19
- BOBBLE [5 DC], PAGE 23
- INVISIBLE DECREASE (INVDEC), PAGE 25

INSTRUCTIONS

HEAD:

Rnd 1: Starting at top of head with A, make an adjustable ring, ch 1, work 6 sc into ring. Pull closed—6 sts. Insert a stitch marker into the loop on your hook. Each time you come back around to the stitch marker, move it up to the loop on your hook to begin the next round.

Rnds 2 and 3: Work 2 sc into each st around—24 sts at end of Rnd 3.

Rnd 4: *2 sc into next st, sc into next st; rep from * to end of rnd—36 sts.

Rnd 5: *2 sc into next st, sc into next 8 sts; rep from * to end of rnd—40 sts.

Rnds 6–9: Sc into each st around.

Rnd 10: *Invdec, sc into next 8 sts; rep from * to end of rnd—36 sts.

Rnd 11: Sc into each st around.

Rnd 12: *Invdec, sc into next 4 sts; rep from * to end of rnd—30 sts.

Rnds 13 and 14: Sc into each st around.

Rnd 15: Sc into next 15 sts, make Bobble in next st (for nose), sc into next 14 sts—30 sts.

Rnd 16: Sc into each st around.

Rnd 17: *Invdec, sc into next 3 sts; rep from * to end of rnd—24 sts.

Rnd 18: Sc into each st around.

Rnd 19: Invdec 3 times, sc into next 12 sts, invdec 3 times—18 sts.

Insert a stitch marker to hold your place. Stuff the head firmly. Insert safety eyes two rounds above bobble and six stitches apart. Continue adding stuffing as you stitch the last couple of rounds if needed.

Rnd 20: Invdec 3 times, sc into next 6 sts, invdec 3 times—12 sts.

Rnd 21: Invdec around—6 sts.

Fasten off with a slip stitch into the next sc and leave a very long tail. Weave yarn tail through the last round of stitches and pull tight to close the hole. Weave tail through to back of the bottom of the head and clip. You will be sewing the head on at a slight angle so that the pointed bottom of the head will create a "chin."

EARS (MAKE 2):

Rnd 1: Starting at edge of ear with A, make an adjustable ring, ch 1, work 6 sc into the ring. Pull closed—6 sts.

Rnd 2: Sc into each st around.

Fasten off with a slip stitch into the next sc and leave a 9"/23cm tail. Use tail to sew ears onto head at eye level on each side of the head.

SHORT AND WIDE MALE HEAD

This is the head to use if you want your male doll to have a more squared-jaw sort of look. Square jaw sounds better than "short and wide," doesn't it?

Materials and Tools

- WORSTED-WEIGHT YARN IN THE FLESH COLOR OF YOUR CHOICE (A) (REFER TO PAGE 12 FOR A LIST OF RECOMMENDED YARNS) (4)
- CROCHET HOOK: 3.5MM (SIZE E-4 U.S.)
- STITCH MARKER
- YARN NEEDLE
- BLACK 10MM SAFETY EYES
- POLYESTER FIBERFILL STUFFING

Stitches and Techniques Used

- ADJUSTABLE RING, PAGE 20
- CHAIN (CH), PAGE 18
- SINGLE CROCHET (SC), PAGE 19
- BOBBLE [5 DC], PAGE 23
- INVISIBLE DECREASE (INVDEC), PAGE 25

INSTRUCTIONS

HEAD:

Rnd 1: Starting at top of head with A, make an adjustable ring, ch 1, work 6 sc into the ring. Pull closed—6 sts. Insert a stitch marker into the loop on your hook. Each time you come back around to the stitch marker, move it up to the loop on your hook to begin the next round.

Rnds 2 and 3: Work 2 sc into each st around—24 sts at end of Rnd 3.

Rnd 4: *2 sc into next st, sc into next st; rep from * to end of rnd—36 sts.

Rnd 5: *2 sc into next st, sc into next 5 sts; rep from * to end of rnd—42 sts.

Rnds 6–8: Sc into each st around.

Rnd 9: *Invdec, sc into next 5 sts; rep from * to end of rnd—36 sts.

Rnds 10 and 11: Sc into each st around.

Rnd 12: *Invdec, sc into next 7 sts; rep from * to end of rnd—32 sts.

Rnd 13: Sc into each st around.

Rnd 14: Sc into next 15 sts, make Bobble in next st (for nose), sc into next 16 sts—32 sts.

Rnds 15 and 16: Sc into each st around.

Rnd 17: Invdec 4 times, sc into next 16 sts, invdec 4 times—24 sts.

Rnd 18: Invdec 3 times, sc into next 12 sts, invdec 3 times—18 sts. Insert a stitch marker to hold your place. Stuff the head firmly. Insert safety eyes two rounds above bobble and six stitches apart. Continue adding stuffing as you stitch the last couple of rounds if needed.

Rnd 19: Invdec 3 times, sc into next 6 sts, invdec 3 times—12 sts.

Rnd 20: Invdec around—6 sts.

Fasten off with a slip stitch into the next sc and leave a very long tail. Weave yarn tail through the last round of stitches and pull tight to close the hole. Weave tail through to back of the bottom of the head and clip. You will be sewing the head on at a slight angle so that the pointed bottom of the head will create a "chin."

EARS (MAKE 2):

Rnd 1: Starting at edge of ear with A, make an adjustable ring, ch 1, work 6 sc into the ring. Pull closed—6 sts.

Rnd 2: Sc into each st around —6 sts.
Fasten off with a slip stitch into the next sc and leave a 9"/23cm tail. Use tail to sew ears onto head at eye level on each side of the head.

LONG AND NARROW FEMALE HEAD

The female heads are shorter than the male heads and have smaller noses, which are crocheted in as you go, as with the male heads. The last few rows form a chin slightly shorter than the chins of the male patterns. This first female head is slightly longer and narrower than the other.

Materials and Tools

- WORSTED-WEIGHT YARN IN THE FLESH COLOR OF YOUR CHOICE (A) (REFER TO PAGE 12 FOR A LIST OF RECOMMENDED YARNS) **(4)**
- CROCHET HOOK: 3.5MM (SIZE E-4 U.S.)
- STITCH MARKER
- YARN NEEDLE
- BLACK 10MM SAFETY EYES
- POLYESTER FIBERFILL STUFFING

Stitches and Techniques Used

- ADJUSTABLE RING, PAGE 20
- CHAIN (CH), PAGE 18
- SINGLE CROCHET (SC), PAGE 19
- BOBBLE (4 DC), PAGE 23
- INVISIBLE DECREASE (INVDEC), PAGE 25

INSTRUCTIONS

HEAD:

Rnd 1: Starting at top of head with A, make an adjustable ring, ch 1, work 6 sc into the ring. Pull closed—6 sts. Insert a stitch marker into the loop on your hook. Each time you come back around to the stitch marker, move it up to the loop on your hook to begin the next round.

Rnd 2: Work 2 sc into each st around—12 sts.

Rnd 3: *2 sc into next st, sc into next st; rep from * to end of rnd —18 sts.

Rnd 4: *2 sc into next st, sc into next 2 sts; rep from * to end of rnd—24 sts.

Rnd 5: *2 sc into next st, sc into next st; rep from * to end of rnd —36 sts.

Rnds 6–8: Sc into each st around.

Rnd 9: [Invdec, sc into next 10 sts] 3 times—33 sts.

Rnd 10: Sc into each st around.

Rnd 11: Sc into next 15 sts, invdec, sc into next 16 sts—32 sts.

Rnd 12: Sc into next 6 sts, invdec, sc into next 24 sts—31 sts.

Rnd 13: Sc into next 23 sts, invdec, sc into next 6 sts—30 sts.

Rnd 14: Sc into next 15 sts, make Bobble into next st (for nose), sc into next 14 sts.

Rnd 15: Sc into each st around.

Rnd 16: [Invdec, sc into next 8 sts] 3 times—27 sts.

Rnd 17: [Sc into next 3 sts, invdec, sc into next 4 sts] 3 times—24 sts.

Rnd 18: Invdec 3 times, sc into next 12 sts, invdec 3 times—18 sts.

Insert a stitch marker to hold your place. Stuff the head firmly. Insert safety eyes positioned two rounds above bobble and six stitches apart. Continue adding stuffing as you stitch the last couple of rounds if needed.

Rnd 19: Invdec 3 times, sc into next 6 sts, invdec 3 times—12 sts.

Rnd 20: Invdec around—6 sts.

Fasten off with a slip stitch into the next sc and leave a very long tail. Weave yarn tail through the last round of stitches and pull tight to close the hole. Weave tail through to back of the bottom of the head and clip. You will be sewing the head on at a slight angle so that the pointed bottom of the head will create a "chin."

EARS (MAKE 2):

Rnd 1: Starting at edge of ear with A, make an adjustable ring, ch 1, work 6 sc into the ring. Pull closed—6 sts.

Rnd 2: Sc into each st around. Fasten off with a slip stitch into the next sc and leave a 9"/23cm tail. Use tail to sew ears onto head at eye level, on each side of the head.

SHORT AND WIDE FEMALE HEAD

This female head is shorter and wider than the other version, with more of a heart shape. The nose is a little smaller than that of the male options.

Materials and Tools

- WORSTED-WEIGHT YARN IN THE FLESH COLOR OF YOUR CHOICE (A) (REFER TO PAGE 12 FOR A LIST OF RECOMMENDED YARNS) (4)
- CROCHET HOOK: 3.5MM (SIZE E-4 U.S.)
- STITCH MARKER
- YARN NEEDLE
- BLACK 10MM SAFETY EYES
- POLYESTER FIBERFILL STUFFING

Stitches and Techniques Used

- ADJUSTABLE RING, PAGE 20
- CHAIN (CH), PAGE 18
- SINGLE CROCHET (SC), PAGE 19
- BOBBLE [4 DC], PAGE 23
- INVISIBLE DECREASE (INVDEC), PAGE 25

INSTRUCTIONS

HEAD:

Rnd 1: Starting at top of head with yarn A, make an adjustable ring, ch 1, work 6 sc into the ring. Pull closed—6 sts. Insert a stitch marker into the loop on your hook. Each time you come back around to the stitch marker, move it up to the loop on your hook to begin the next round.

Rnds 2 and 3: Work 2 sc into each st around—24 sts at end of Rnd 3.

Rnd 4: *2 sc into next st, sc into next st; rep from * to end of rnd—36 sts.

Rnd 5: *2 sc into next st, sc into next 5 sts; rep from * to end of rnd—42 sts.

Rnds 6 and 7: Sc into each st around.

Rnd 8: *Invdec, sc into next 5 sts; rep from * to end of rnd—36 sts.

Rnd 9: *Invdec, sc into next 4 sts; rep from * to end of rnd—30 sts.

Rnds 10 and 11: Sc into each st around.

Rnd 12: Sc into next 15 sts, make Bobble into next st (for nose), sc into next 14 sts.

Rnd 13: *Invdec, sc into next 3 sts; rep from * to end of rnd—24 sts.

Rnd 14: Sc into each st around.

Rnd 15: Invdec 3 times, sc into next 12 sts, invdec 3 times—18 sts. Insert a stitch marker to hold your place. Stuff the head firmly. Insert safety eyes positioned as shown.

Continue adding stuffing as you stitch the last couple of rounds if needed.

Rnd 16: Invdec 3 times, sc into next 6 sts, invdec 3 times—12 sts.

Rnd 17: Invdec around—6 sts. Fasten off with a slip stitch into the next sc and leave a very long tail. Weave yarn tail through the last round of stitches and pull tight to close the hole. Weave tail through to back of the bottom of the head and clip. You will be sewing the head on at a slight angle so that the pointed bottom of the head will create a "chin."

EARS (MAKE 2):

Rnd 1: Starting at edge of ear with A, make an adjustable ring, ch 1, work 6 sc into the ring. Pull closed—6 sts.

Rnd 2: Sc into each st around—6 sts.

Fasten off with a slip stitch into the next sc and leave a 9"/23cm tail. Use tail to sew ears onto head at eye level, on each side of the head.

BASIC CHILD'S HEAD

While making dolls that look like grownups is fun, when you give a child a doll that looks like him (or her), you'll get to see some real excitement! This first child's head pattern is basically a scaled-down version of an adult head. Use smaller 6mm eyes for a smaller head. The bobble stitch used in the nose will be smaller.

Materials and Tools

- WORSTED-WEIGHT YARN IN THE FLESH COLOR OF YOUR CHOICE (A) (REFER TO PAGE 12 FOR A LIST OF RECOMMENDED YARNS) (4)
- CROCHET HOOK: 3.5MM (SIZE E-4 U.S.)
- STITCH MARKER
- YARN NEEDLE
- BLACK 6MM SAFETY EYES
- POLYESTER FIBERFILL STUFFING

Stitches and Techniques Used

- ADJUSTABLE RING, PAGE 20
- CHAIN (CH), PAGE 18
- SINGLE CROCHET (SC), PAGE 19
- BOBBLE [3 DC], PAGE 23
- INVISIBLE DECREASE (INVDEC), PAGE 25

INSTRUCTIONS

HEAD:

Rnd 1: Starting at top of head with A, make an adjustable ring, ch 1, work 6 sc into the ring. Pull closed—6 sts. Insert a stitch marker into the loop on your hook. Each time you come back around to the stitch marker, move it up to the loop on your hook to begin the next round.

Rnds 2 and 3: Work 2 sc into each st around—24 sts at end of Rnd 3.

Rnds 4–7: Sc into each st around.

Rnd 8: Invdec, sc into next 22 sts —23 sts.

Rnd 9: Invdec, sc into next 10 sts, make Bobble into next st (for nose), sc into next 10 sts—22 sts.

Rnd 10: [Sc into next 5 sts, 2 sc in next st, sc into next 5 sts] twice —24 sts.

Rnd 11: Sc into each st around.

Rnd 12: Invdec 3 times, sc into next 12 sts, invdec 3 times—18 sts.

Rnd 13: Invdec 3 times, sc into next 6 sts, invdec 3 times—12 sts.

Insert a stitch marker to hold your place. Stuff the head firmly. Insert safety eyes one round above bobble, four stitches apart. Stuff firmly and continue, adding stuffing at the end if needed.

Rnd 14: Invdec around—6 sts.

Fasten off with a slip stitch into the next sc and leave a very long tail. Weave yarn tail through the last round of stitches and pull tight to close the hole. Weave tail through to back of the bottom of the head and clip. You will be sewing the head on at a slight angle so that the pointed bottom of the head will create a "chin."

EARS (MAKE 2):

Rnd 1: Starting at edge of ear with A, make an adjustable ring, ch 1, work 5 sc into the ring. Pull closed—5 sts.

Rnd 2: Sc into each st around. Fasten off with a slip stitch into the next sc and leave a 9"/23cm tail. Use tail to sew ears onto head at eye level, on each side of the head.

WIDE AND ROUND CHILD'S HEAD

Instead of a mini-adult head, this kid-size head is more cartoonlike in proportion. The bobble stitch has been adjusted for a small, child-size nose.

Materials and Tools

■ WORSTED-WEIGHT YARN IN THE FLESH COLOR OF YOUR CHOICE (A) (REFER TO PAGE 12 FOR A LIST OF RECOMMENDED YARNS) **(4)**

■ CROCHET HOOK: 3.5MM (SIZE E-4 U.S.)

■ STITCH MARKER

■ YARN NEEDLE

■ BLACK 6MM SAFETY EYES

■ POLYESTER FIBERFILL STUFFING

Stitches and Techniques Used

■ ADJUSTABLE RING, PAGE 20

■ CHAIN (CH), PAGE 18

■ SINGLE CROCHET (SC), PAGE 19

■ BOBBLE [3 DC], PAGE 23

■ INVISIBLE DECREASE (INVDEC), PAGE 25

INSTRUCTIONS
HEAD:

Rnd 1: Starting at top of head with A, make an adjustable ring, ch 1, work 6 sc into the ring. Pull closed—6 sts. Insert a stitch marker into the loop on your hook. Each time you come back around to the stitch marker, move it up to the loop on your hook to begin the next round.

Rnds 2 and 3: Work 2 sc into each st around—24 sts at end of Rnd 3.

Rnd 4: *2 sc into next st, sc into next 3 sts; rep from * to end of rnd—30 sts.

Rnd 5: Sc into each st around.

Rnd 6: [Invdec, sc into next 13 sts] twice—28 sts.

Rnd 7: [Sc into next 5 sts, invdec, sc into next 7 sts] twice—26 sts.

Rnd 8: Sc into next 12 sts, invdec, sc into next 12 sts—25 sts.

Rnd 9: Invdec, sc into each st around—24 sts.

Rnd 10: Invdec, sc into next 10 sts, make Bobble in next st (for nose), sc into next 11 sts—23 sts.

Rnd 11: Sc into next 10 sts, invdec, sc into next 11 sts—22 sts.

Rnd 12: Sc into next 4 sts, invdec, sc into next 10 sts, invdec, sc into next 4 sts—20 sts.

Rnd 13: Invdec 4 times, sc into next 4 sts, invdec 4 times—12 sts.

Insert a stitch marker to hold your place. Stuff the head firmly. Insert safety eyes one row above bobble, four stitches apart. Stuff firmly and continue, adding stuffing at the end if needed.

Rnd 14: Invdec around—6 sts.

Fasten off with a slip stitch into the next sc and leave a very long tail. Weave yarn tail through the last round of stitches and pull tight to close the hole. Weave tail through to back of the bottom of the head. You will be sewing the head on at a slight angle so that the pointed bottom of the head will create a "chin."

EARS (MAKE 2):

Rnd 1: Starting at edge of ear with A, make an adjustable ring, ch 1, work 5 sc into the ring. Pull closed—5 sts.

Rnd 2: Sc into each st around.

Fasten off with a slip stitch into the next sc and leave a 9"/23cm tail. Use tail to sew ears onto head at eye level, on each side of the head.

EMBROIDERING A FACE

Take a look at that expressionless face on the head you just made. Lifeless. No personality. Just a couple of eyes. You can change that! Think of the face as a blank canvas. Embroidering your doll's face is the first step in bringing your creation to life. A few stitches with an embroidery needle can quickly and easily transform your doll into a unique being.

From making so many look-alike dolls, I've come up with a quick trick to make faces recognizable. Look at pictures of your subject. Lots of pictures. A quick Google image search should yield many photos if you're making a famous person. You'll find that someone smiling almost always makes the same expression. Does he always have his mouth open? Do her eyes squint? Do his teeth show? Are they top or bottom teeth and do they touch or set apart? Does she almost always wear bright pink or red lipstick? Maybe the person barely ever smiles. While you might not want to make a doll with a perpetual frown, a more serious expression may suit the person's character. Don't turn up both edges of that embroidered mouth. Make the eyebrows slant inward slightly. Use these subtle clues to form the little details that will add life to your doll.

I always sketch out the face before even threading my needle. Using a pencil, draw a simple oval and add the basic eyes and nose, then start experimenting. Sketch different eyebrows, add eyelashes, and draw and erase mouths until you feel you've got the person's expression the way you want it. Ask for someone else's opinion. Several times I've been satisfied with a face and asked for feedback from my husband or even my kids, and they've given me pointers on a minor change that made all the difference. Bushier eyebrows, an extra embroidered line below the bottom lip, or just a mole you didn't notice can all make a big difference.

Listed below are several options for your doll's face and the embroidery stitches you'll need.

Straight stitch or stem stitch:
- EYEBROWS
- EYELASHES (EASILY FEMINIZES A FACE)
- MOUTH (SMILE, FROWN, SMIRK, HALF-SMILE)
- DIMPLES (TINY STITCHES AROUND THE MOUTH WITH BLACK THREAD)
- WRINKLES (A DARKER FLESH-TONED THREAD WORKS BEAUTIFULLY FOR THIS)

French knot:
- FRECKLES
- MOLE/BEAUTY MARK

Don't forget to vary the color of your stitches. Almost every doll can have black eyelashes but stitching red lines above and below a black line creates a very feminine mouth. Using brown or gold for eyebrows looks more natural for a brunette or blonde.

OTHER OPTIONS

While using embroidery floss is an obvious choice for embroidering thin lines on your doll's face, what about when you want a fuller lip or an open mouth?

YARN
You can use scraps of pink or red yarn to create a full lip. Loose straight stitches using yarn and a yarn needle make a doll's mouth stand out. Instead of embroidery floss for eyebrows, use the same yarn you plan to use for the doll's hair. The brows will be slightly bushier and a perfect match. Separate plies of yarn can be used for a thinner brow.

FELT
In addition to using embroidery floss and yarn to embroider features, felt can sometimes add the perfect touch.

If a doll has an open mouth, nothing works better than a scrap of black felt, cut into the shape of a smile, glued or stitched to the doll's face. Add a small strip of white felt on top for teeth. Pay special attention to the shape of the teeth if you add them. A space between teeth will add instant character. With just a few snips of your detail scissors you can really make a difference. Make sure the felt lies flat when you layer it. Press layers together firmly.

Lip service? Use felt for a smile, then outline with pink or red yarn for a full lip and open-mouthed smile. For a more natural look but maintaining fuller lips, use yarn slightly darker than the skin-tone yarn you are using.

FINISHING
Adding a little color to your doll's face can sometimes really brighten him or her up. Maybe he or she looks a little pale? Add pink or peach blush to the cheeks for a rosy glow. A tiny bit of eyeshadow over your doll's eyes will add a neat detail. Even crayons in vibrant colors can be used for bold eye looks. Brown or black mascara gently dabbed on the chin and face makes a great stubbly five o'clock shadow. Make sure any makeup you use on the doll is applied very lightly. Over time, powdery blushes and eye shadows may fade. Mascara used on the doll should be allowed to dry completely before handling. Less is definitely more in this case!

UPPER BODY

Now that your doll has a head, the next step is the body and arms. This is where things get interesting. They say clothes make the man (or woman, or kid, for that matter). Think about that for a moment. You're making the clothes AND the man! You'll dress up your doll how you want him or her to look, be it casual, formal, sporty, for cold weather or warm weather, for work or play. Each choice you make will determine your doll's character, interests, and overall look.

To make an upper body—which includes the torso and arms—you'll need to choose a top from the first four patterns. Just four patterns, you say? Well, actually, there are way more than just these four options. Each of the patterns, depending on the colors you choose, the embellishments you add, and the way you decide to crochet them, will provide dozens of options. Within each pattern, you can choose sleeve length and sizing. There's no need to crochet only basic shirts with one color. Create stripes by changing colors every few rows or use a variegated yarn for a patterned look. After crocheting a basic top, you can add a felt shape to the front to make a graphic T. Embroider a name for personalization. Shirt tucked in or untucked? Rolled-up cuffs or wide collar? Decide which your doll prefers and crochet it that way.

Also, I've noticed some dolls just look better dressed up! So there are also instructions in this chapter for "outerwear." The outerwear is optional and made to layer over one of the three basic upper bodies.

If you're making a male or female adult doll, complete the patterns as written. The first top pattern includes instructions for making muscular arms, too, if your doll wants to be a little more buff. Look for the special child-size patterns if you're making a child-size doll.

BASIC TOP

The first upper-body pattern is for a basic top. It is the basis for many options: short sleeves, long sleeves, and ³/₄-length sleeves are all options. And any version can be embellished to make graphic Ts, striped for alternating colors (using the "Changing Color" instructions on page 29), or made entirely in the main flesh color for the doll to remain shirtless.

The body will be crocheted first—the bottom up to the neck (which is left open for sewing to the head). Arms are crocheted separately and sewn on. If your doll has meatier, more muscular arms, there's a separate pattern for those, too! Instructions are provided after the pattern for assembling the doll pieces. For a Child's Basic Top, follow the separate pattern instructions.

Materials and Tools

- WORSTED-WEIGHT YARN IN THE SHIRT COLOR(S) (A) AND FLESH COLOR (B) OF YOUR CHOICE (REFER TO PAGE 12 FOR A LIST OF RECOMMENDED YARNS) **4**
- CROCHET HOOK: 3.5MM (SIZE E-4 U.S.)
- STITCH MARKER
- YARN NEEDLE
- POLYESTER FIBERFILL STUFFING
- NARROW WOODEN DOWEL, 6"/15CM LONG

Stitches and Techniques Used

- ADJUSTABLE RING, PAGE 20
- CHAIN (CH), PAGE 18
- SINGLE CROCHET (SC), PAGE 19
- BOBBLE (5 DC), PAGE 23
- INVISIBLE DECREASE (INVDEC), PAGE 25
- SURFACE SINGLE CROCHET (SURFACE SC), PAGE 30

INSTRUCTIONS FOR ADULT

Rnd 1: Starting at bottom of body with A, make an adjustable ring, ch 1, work 6 sc into the ring. Pull closed—6 sts.

Rnds 2 and 3: Work 2 sc into each st around—24 sts at end of Rnd 3.

Rnds 4–17: Sc into each st around.

Rnd 18: Invdec around—12 sts.

Insert a stitch marker to hold your place. Stuff body. Continue crocheting, stuffing a little more as needed.

Rnd 19: [Invdec, sc into next 2 sts] 3 times; change to B—9 sts.

Rnds 20 and 21: Sc into each st around—9 sts.

Fasten off with a slip stitch into the next sc and leave a long tail for sewing to the head. Insert a wooden dowel into the head a few rounds behind the base round of stitches on the bottom of the head. Insert the other end into the top of the body you have just made. Use the tail to sew the body to the head around the dowel. The dowel will support the weight of the head on top of the skinny neck of the doll. See page 31 for more information on this technique.

BASIC ARMS (MAKE 2):

These are the arms you see in the photo at far right. For long sleeves, change to A at Rnd 6. For ¾ length, change color at Rnd 11. For short sleeves, change color at Rnd 16.

Rnd 1: Starting at hand end of arm with B, make an adjustable ring, ch 1, work 4 sc into the ring. Pull closed—4 sts.

Rnd 2: Work 2 sc into each st around—8 sts.

Rnds 3 and 4: Sc in each sc around.

Rnd 5: Sc in next 3 sc, make Bobble in next sc (for thumb), sc in next 2 sc, invdec—7 sts.

Rnds 6–19: Sc in each sc around.

Rnd 20: Invdec, sc in each sc around—6 sts.

Fasten off with a slip stitch into the next sc and leave a long tail. Stuff arms sparingly. Use the eraser end of a pencil to gently push small bits of stuffing toward the hand end. Too much stuffing will make the arms stand out straight from the body. Weave yarn tail through the last round of stitches and pull tight to shrink opening at the top of the arm. Make arms poseable using instructions on page 16 and sew the arms to the body at the shoulder.

MUSCULAR ARMS

MUSCULAR ARMS (MAKE 2):

These buffed-up arms can be used for male or female dolls. Follow the same pattern for color changes in Basic Arms. For long sleeves, change to A at Rnd 6. For ¾ length, change color at Rnd 11. For short sleeves, change color at Rnd 16.

Rnd 1: Starting at hand end of arm with B, make an adjustable ring, ch 1, work 4 sc into the ring. Pull closed—4 sts.

Rnd 2: Work 2 sc into each st around—8 sts.

Rnds 3 and 4: Sc in each sc around.

Rnd 5: Sc in next 3 sc, work Bobble in next sc (for thumb), sc in next 2 sc, invdec—7 sts.

Rnds 6–9: Sc in each sc around.

Rnd 10: Work 2 sc in next st, sc into each st around—8 sts.

Rnds 11–13: Sc in each st around.

Rnd 14: [Invdec, sc in next 2 sts] twice—6 sts.

Rnd 15: [2 sc in next st, sc into next 2 sts] twice—8 sts.

Rnd 16: Sc in next 4 sts, 2 sc in next st, sc in next 3 sts—9 sts.

Rnd 17: Work 2 sc in next st, sc into each st around—10 sts.

Rnd 18: [2 sc in next st, sc into next 4 sts] twice—12 sts.

Rnd 19: Sc in each st around.

Rnd 20: [Invdec, sc in next 2 sts] 3 times—9 sts.

Rnd 21: [Invdec, sc in next sc] 3 times—6 sts.

Fasten off with a slip stitch into the next sc and leave a long tail. Stuff arms to fill out muscles. Use the eraser end of a pencil to gently push small bits of stuffing toward the hand end. Weave yarn tail through the last round of stitches and pull tight to shrink opening at the top of the arm. Make arms poseable using instructions on page 16 and sew the arms to the body at the shoulder.

CUFFS (MAKE 2):

The cuffs are crocheted separately and added to the arms, either at the wrist or at the elbow, where you have made a color change for the transition to the shirt.

Row 1: Beginning at the bottom edge of the cuff with A, ch 10, sc in 2nd ch from hook and next 8 ch—9 sts.

(If you are making cuffs to add to a child's shirt, fasten off after Row 1 and sew to arms.)

Row 2: Ch 1, turn, sc in each sc across.

Fasten off, leaving a long tail for sewing. Sew bottom edge of cuff to arm at color change, starting and ending at the outside of arm. Weave in ends.

SHIRTTAIL:

If you'd like your doll to have his or her shirt untucked, make a shirttail. It is crocheted directly onto the body at the waist, around Rnd 6.

Rnd 1: Turn body upside down, with A, work surface sc all the way around Rnd 6 of body—24 sts.

Rnd 2: [2 sc into next sc, sc into next 11 sc] twice—26 sts.

Rnds 3–6: Sc into each sc around.

Continue for additional rounds if desired, which will make the shirttail longer. Fasten off with a slip stitch into the next sc. Weave in ends.

INSTRUCTIONS FOR CHILD

Rnd 1: Starting at bottom of body with A, make an adjustable ring, ch 1, work 6 sc into the ring. Pull closed—6 sts.

Rnd 2: Work 2 sc into each st around—12 sts.

Rnd 3: *2 sc into next st, sc into next st; rep from * to end of rnd —18 sts.

Rnd 4: [2 sc into next st, sc into next 8 sts] twice—20 sts.

Rnds 5–14: Sc into each st around.

Rnd 15: Invdec around—10 sts.

Change to B at the end of Rnd 15. Insert a stitch marker to hold your place. Stuff the body firmly.

Rnd 16: [Invdec, sc into next 3 sts] twice—8 sts.

Rnd 17: Sc into each st around.

Fasten off with a slip stitch into the next sc and leave a long tail for sewing to the head. Insert wooden dowel into the head a few rounds behind the base round of stitches on the bottom of the head. Insert the other end into the top of the body you have just made. Use tail to sew body to head around the dowel. The dowel will support the weight of the head on top of the skinny neck of the doll. See page 31 for more information on this technique.

CHILD'S ARMS (MAKE 2):

For long sleeves, change to A at Rnd 6. For ¾ length, change color at Rnd 9. For short sleeves, change color at Rnd 12.

Rnd 1: Starting at hand end of arm with B, make an adjustable ring, ch 1, work 4 sc into the ring. Pull closed—4 sts.

Rnd 2: Work 2 sc into each st around—8 sts.

Rnds 3 and 4: Sc in each sc around.

Rnd 5: Sc in next 3 sc, make Bobble in next sc (for thumb), sc in next 2 sc, invdec—7 sts.

Rnds 6–14: Sc in each sc around.

Rnd 15: Invdec, sc in each sc around—6 sts.

Fasten off with a slip stitch into the next sc and leave a long tail. Stuff arms sparingly. Use the eraser end of a pencil to gently push small bits of stuffing toward the hand end. Too much stuffing will make the arms stand out straight from the body. Weave yarn tail through the last round of stitches and pull tight to shrink opening at the top of the arm. Make arms poseable using instructions on page 16 and sew the arms to the body at the shoulder.

CHILD'S CUFFS (MAKE 2):

Follow the instructions for cuffs on page 45.

CHILD'S SHIRTTAIL:

Kids rarely keep their shirts tucked in. The optional shirttail is crocheted directly onto the body at the waist, around Rnd 5. Crochet the foundation round into the loops on the surface of each stitch around in a spiral.

Rnd 1: Turn body upside down. With A, make a slip knot and place it on your hook. Insert your hook into the loop of a st in Rnd 5 of the body and make a sc, work a sc into the loop of each remaining st around—20 sts.

Rnd 2: [2 sc into next sc, sc into next 9 sc] twice—22 sts.

Rnds 3 and 4: Sc into each sc around.

Continue for additional rounds if desired, which will make the shirttail longer. Fasten off with a slip stitch into the next sc. Weave in ends.

COLLARED TOP

The next pattern for the upper body has a polo-style collar. Optional short sleeves are worked separately. Instead of the separate short sleeves, you can make long sleeves, or cuffs crocheted separately. They can be sewn on at the elbow to mimic rolled-up sleeves or at the wrist for a French-cuff dress shirt with cufflinks. You can even add a necktie (page 51) for complete business attire! The body will be crocheted first—the bottom up to the neck (which is left open for sewing to the head). Arms are crocheted separately and sewn on. For a Child's Collared Top, follow the instructions within the pattern for fewer repeating rounds and shorter arms. Instructions are provided after the pattern for assembling the doll pieces.

Materials and Tools

- WORSTED-WEIGHT YARN IN THE SHIRT COLOR(S) (A) AND FLESH COLOR (B) OF YOUR CHOICE (REFER TO PAGE 12 FOR A LIST OF RECOMMENDED YARNS) **(4)**
- CROCHET HOOK: 3.5MM (SIZE E-4 U.S.)
- STITCH MARKER
- YARN NEEDLE
- POLYESTER FIBERFILL STUFFING
- NARROW WOODEN DOWEL, 6"/15CM LONG

Stitches and Techniques Used

- ADJUSTABLE RING, PAGE 20
- CHAIN (CH), PAGE 18
- SINGLE CROCHET (SC), PAGE 19
- DOUBLE CROCHET (DC), PAGE 22
- BOBBLE [5 DC], PAGE 23
- INVISIBLE DECREASE (INVDEC), PAGE 25

INSTRUCTIONS FOR aDULT

Rnd 1: Starting at bottom of body with A, make an adjustable ring, ch 1, work 6 sc into the ring. Pull closed—6 sts.

Rnds 2 and 3: Work 2 sc into each st around—24 sts at end of Rnd 3.

Rnds 4–17: Sc into each st around.

Rnd 18: Invdec around—12 sts.

Insert a stitch marker to hold your place. Stuff body. Continue crocheting, stuffing a little more as needed. The collar will be created now.

Row 19: Ch 2 (does not count as st), turn, dc into next st, sc into next 10 sts, dc into next st—12 sts.

Row 20: Ch 1, turn, sc into next 12 sts.

Fasten off and leave a 9"/23cm tail. Use tail to sew collar down around the top of the body piece. Weave in end. This has created a collar around the top of the shirt.

Draw up a loop of B in the middle unworked back loop of Rnd 17 at center of back neck.

Rnd 21: Invdec around—12 sts.

Rnd 22: [Invdec, sc into next 2 sts] 3 times—9 sts.

Rnds 23 and 24: Sc into each st around.

Fasten off with a slip stitch into the next sc and leave a long tail for sewing to the head. Insert wooden dowel into the head a few rounds behind the base round of stitches on the bottom of the head. Insert the other end into the top of the body you have just made. Use tail to sew body to head around the dowel. The dowel will support the weight of the head on top of the skinny neck of the doll. See page 31 for more information on this technique.

ARMS (MAKE 2):

For long sleeves, change to A at Rnd 7. For ¾ length, change color at Rnd 11. For short sleeves, you will work the entire sleeve with B, then create the short sleeves separately, below.

Rnd 1: Starting at hand end of arm with B, make an adjustable ring, ch 1, work 4 sc into the ring. Pull closed—4 sts.

Rnd 2: Work 2 sc into each st around—8 sts.

Rnds 3 and 4: Sc in each sc around.

Rnd 5: Sc in next 3 sc, make Bobble in next sc (for thumb), sc in next 2 sc, invdec—7 sts.

Rnds 6–19: Sc in each sc around.

Rnd 20: Invdec, sc in each sc around—6 sts.

Fasten off with a slip stitch into the next sc and leave a long tail. Stuff arms sparingly. Use the eraser end of a pencil to gently push small bits of stuffing toward the hand end. Too much stuffing will make the arms stand out straight from the body. Weave yarn tail through the last round of stitches and pull tight to shrink opening at the top of the arm. Make arms poseable using instructions on page 16. Make Cuffs or Short Sleeves and sew the arms to the body at the shoulder.

CUFFS (MAKE 2):

The cuffs are crocheted separately and added to the arms, either at the wrist or at the elbow, where you have made a color change for the transition to the shirt.

Row 1: Beginning at the bottom edge of the cuff with A, ch 10, sc in 2nd ch from hook and next 8 ch—9 sts.

(If you are making cuffs to add to a child's shirt, fasten off after Row 1 and sew to arms.)

Row 2: Ch 1, turn, sc in each sc across.

Fasten off, leaving a long tail for sewing. Sew bottom edge of cuff to arm at color change, starting and ending at the outside of arm. Weave in ends.

SHORT OR LONG SLEEVE (MAKE 2):

An alternate short sleeve will be crocheted separately and fit over the top of the arm. It will be sewn on before sewing the completed arm and sleeve to the body.

Rnd 1: Starting at shoulder of sleeve with A, make an adjustable ring, ch 1, work 6 sc into the ring. Pull closed—6 sts.

Rnd 2: [2 sc into next st, sc into next st] 3 times—9 sts.

Rnds 3–5: Sc into each st around.

For longer sleeves, continue for as many rounds as desired. Increasing each round by one stitch will create full sleeves. Crocheting these longer sleeves in a lighter, sport-weight yarn will make them softer and flowing.

Fasten off with a slip stitch into the next sc and leave a long tail. Weave the yarn tail up through sleeve to the top opening. Insert stuffed arm into sleeve and use the sleeve's yarn tail to sew the sleeve into place at the top of the arm. Position assembled arm into place on the body and use the sleeve's yarn tail to sew the assembled arm to body. Hide yarn tail within body.

SHIRTTAIL:

If your doll's shirt is untucked, crochet a Shirttail (page 45).

INSTRUCTIONS FOR CHILD

Rnd 1: Starting at bottom of body with A, make an adjustable ring, ch 1, work 6 sc into the ring. Pull closed—6 sts.

Rnd 2: Work 2 sc into each st around—12 sts.

Rnd 3: *2 sc into next st, sc into next st; rep from * to end of rnd —18 sts.

Rnd 4: [2 sc into next st, sc into next 8 sts] twice—20 sts.

Rnds 5–14: Sc into each st around.

Rnd 15: Invdec around—10 sts. Insert a stitch marker to hold your place. Stuff body. Continue crocheting, stuffing a little more as needed. The collar will be created now.

Rnd 16: Ch 3, turn, dc into next st, sc into next 8 sts, dc into next st—12 sts.

Rnd 17: Ch 1, turn, sc into next 12 sts.

Fasten off with a slip stitch into the next sc and leave a 9"/23cm tail. Use tail to sew collar down around the top of the body piece. Weave in end. This has created a collar around the top of the shirt.

Draw up a loop of B in the middle unworked back loop of Rnd 14 at center of back neck.

Rnd 18: Invdec around—10 sts.

Rnd 19: [Invdec, sc into next 3 sts] twice—8 sts.

Rnds 20 and 21: Sc into each st around.

Fasten off with a slip stitch into the next sc and leave a long tail for sewing to the head. Insert wooden dowel into the head a few rounds behind the base round of stitches on the bottom of the head. Insert the other end into the top of the body you have just made. Use tail to sew body to head around the dowel. The dowel will support the weight of the head on top of the skinny neck of the doll. See page 31 for more information on this technique.

CHILD'S ARMS (MAKE 2):

For long sleeves, change to A at Rnd 6. For ¾ sleeves, change color after Rnd 10. For short sleeves, change color at Rnd 12 or crochet separate Short Sleeves, below.

Rnd 1: Starting at hand end of arm with B, make an adjustable ring, ch 1, work 4 sc into the ring. Pull closed—4 sts.

Rnd 2: Work 2 sc into each st around—8 sts.

Rnds 3 and 4: Sc in each sc around.

Rnd 5: Sc in next 3 sc, make Bobble in next sc (for thumb), sc in next 2 sc, invdec—7 sts.

Rnds 6–14: Sc in each sc around.

Rnd 15: Invdec, sc in each sc around—6 sts.

Fasten off with a slip stitch into the next sc and leave a long tail. Stuff arms sparingly. Use the eraser end of a pencil to gently push small bits of stuffing toward the hand end. Too much stuffing will make the arms stand out straight from the body. Weave yarn tail through the last round of stitches and pull tight to shrink opening at the top of the arm. Make optional Cuffs or Short Sleeve, below. Make arms poseable using instructions on page 16 and sew the arms to the body at the shoulder.

CHILD'S CUFFS (MAKE 2):

Follow the instructions for cuffs on page 45.

CHILD'S SHORT OR LONG SLEEVE (MAKE 2):

The short sleeve will be crocheted separately and fit over the top of the arm. It will be sewn on before sewing the completed arm and sleeve to the body.

Rnd 1: Starting at shoulder of sleeve with A, make an adjustable ring, ch 1, work 6 sc into the ring. Pull closed—6 sts.

Rnd 2: [2 sc into next st, sc into next st] 3 times—9 sts.

Rnds 3 and 4: Sc into each st around.

Fasten off with a slip stitch into the next sc and leave a long tail. Weave the yarn tail up through sleeve to the top opening. Insert stuffed arm into sleeve and use the sleeve's yarn tail to sew the sleeve into place at the top. Position arm into place on the body and use the sleeve's yarn tail to sew arm to body. Hide yarn tail within body.

SHIRTTAIL:

If your doll's shirt is untucked, crochet a Shirttail (page 45).

Ties For Guys

NECKTIE:

Let's get down to business! A necktie fancies this look up, and is quick and easy to make.

Row 1: With desired worsted weight yarn, ch 4, sc into 2nd ch from hook and next 2 ch—3 sts.

Row 2: Ch 1, turn, sc3tog—1 st.

Row 3: Ch 1, turn, 2 sc into st —2 sts.

Row 4: Ch 1, turn, sc into each st across.

Row 5: Ch 1, turn, 2 sc into next st, sc into next st—3 sts.

Rows 6–10: Ch 1, turn, sc into each st across.

Row 11: Ch 1, turn, sc into next st, 2 sc into next st, sc into last st— 4 sts.

Row 12: Ch 1, turn, c into each st across.

Row 13: Ch 1, turn, invdec across—2 sts.

Row 14: Ch 1, turn, invdec— 1 st. Fasten off and leave a long tail. Embroider stripes if you'd like with embroidery floss. Weave yarn tail up through tie to the top and sew onto doll's shirt at the collar.

BOWTIE:

If your doll needs to dress in formal attire, he needs a bowtie. Maybe he marches to the beat of a different drummer, is an intellectual, or wants to stand out in the crowd. A quick-to-crochet bowtie creates an instant defining look.

Row 1: With desired worsted weight yarn, ch 4, sc into 2nd ch from hook and each ch across, ch 1, turn—3 sts.

Row 2: Invdec, sc into next st —2 sts.

Row 3: Ch 1, turn, sc into each st across.

Row 4: Ch 1, turn, invdec—1 st.

Row 5: Ch 1, turn, 2 sc into next st—2 sts.

Row 6: Ch 1, turn, 2 sc into next st, sc into next st—3 sts.

Row 7: Ch 1, turn, sc into each st across.

Fasten off, leaving a long tail. Weave long tail through to middle of bowtie. Wrap center of bowtie with yarn tail and then weave tail back into bowtie. Use the yarn tail to sew the bowtie to collar. Weave starting tail through bowtie and hide it within body.

CURVY TOP

This top is strictly feminine. Because it is a more grown-up shape, there isn't a child's version. The main body is crocheted in the shirt color of your choice, with a color change near the top for the neckline. For an untucked top, instructions are included for a shirttail. Change color on the arms for ³/₄-length sleeves and add a folded cuff if you want to!

Materials and Tools

■ WORSTED-WEIGHT YARN IN TOP COLOR (A) AND FLESH COLOR (B) OF YOUR CHOICE (REFER TO PAGE 12 FOR A LIST OF RECOMMENDED YARNS) **(4)**
■ CROCHET HOOK: 3.5MM (SIZE E-4 U.S.)
■ STITCH MARKER
■ YARN NEEDLE
■ POLYESTER FIBERFILL STUFFING
■ NARROW WOODEN DOWEL, 6"/15CM LONG

Stitches and Techniques Used

■ ADJUSTABLE RING, PAGE 20
■ CHAIN (CH), PAGE 18
■ SINGLE CROCHET (SC), PAGE 19
■ HALF DOUBLE CROCHET (HDC), PAGE 21
■ INVISIBLE DECREASE (INVDEC), PAGE 25
■ BOBBLE (5 DC), PAGE 23

INSTRUCTIONS

Rnd 1: Starting at bottom of body with A, make an adjustable ring, ch 1, work 6 sc into the ring. Pull closed—6 sts.

Rnds 2 and 3: Work 2 sc into each st around—24 sts at end of Rnd 3.

Rnds 4–6: Sc into each st around.

Rnd 7: [Invdec, sc into next 6 sts] 3 times—21 sts.

Rnd 8: [Invdec, sc into next 5 sts] 3 times—18 sts.

Rnds 9 and 10: Sc into each st around.

Rnd 11: Work 2 sc into next st, sc into each st around—19 sts.

Rnd 12: Sc into each st around.

Rnd 13: Work 2 sc into next st, sc into each st around—20 sts.

Rnd 14: Sc into each st around.

Rnd 15: *2 sc into next st, sc into next 4 sts; rep from * to end of rnd—24 sts.

Rnd 16: Sc into next 10 sts, 2 hdc into each of next 2 sts, sc into next st, 2 hdc into each of next 2 sts, sc into next 9 sts—28 sts.

Rnd 17: Sc into next 8 sts, invdec 3 times, sc into next st, invdec 3 times, sc into next 7 sts—22 sts.

Rnd 18: Sc into next 6 sts, invdec, sc into next 7 sts, invdec, sc into next 5 sts; change to B—20 sts.

Rnd 19: Invdec around—10 sts. Insert a stitch marker to hold your place. Stuff body. Continue crocheting, stuffing a little more as needed.

Rnd 20: Sc into next 4 sts, invdec, sc into next 4 sts—9 sts.

Rnds 21 and 22: Sc into each st around.

Fasten off with a slip stitch into the next sc and leave a long tail for sewing to the head. Insert a wooden dowel into the head a few rounds behind the base round of stitches on the bottom of the head. Insert the other end into the top of the body you have just made. Use tail to sew body to head around the dowel. The dowel will support the weight of the head on top of the skinny neck of the doll. See page 31 for more information on this technique.

COLLAR:

To dress up the doll's top, add a collar. It's crocheted separately and sewn on.

Row 1: With A, ch 15, 2 sc in 2nd ch from hook, sc in next 12 ch, 2 sc in last ch—16 sts.

Row 2: Ch 2, turn, hdc in each st across.

Fasten off, leaving a long tail for sewing. Beginning and ending at center front, sew collar around neck.

SHIRTTAIL:

If you'd like your doll to have her shirt untucked, make a Shirttail (page 45).

ARMS (MAKE 2):

For ¾ sleeve tops, change to A at the end of Rnd 10. For short sleeves, change color at the end of Rnd 15. Dolls with sleeveless tops will have arms crocheted entirely in flesh-toned B.

Rnd 1: Starting at hand end of arm with B, make an adjustable ring, ch 1, work 4 sc into the ring. Pull closed—4 sts.

Rnd 2: Work 2 sc into each st around—8 sts.

Rnds 3 and 4: Sc in each sc around.

Rnd 5: Sc in next 3 sc, make Bobble in next sc (for thumb), sc in next 2 sc, invdec—7 sts.

Rnds 6–19: Sc in each sc around.

Rnd 20: Invdec, sc in each sc around—6 sts.

Fasten off with a slip stitch into the next sc and leave a long tail. Stuff arms sparingly. Use the eraser end of a pencil to gently push small bits of stuffing toward the hand end. Too much stuffing will make the arms stand out straight from the body. Weave yarn tail through the last round of stitches and pull tight to shrink opening at the top of the arm. Make arms poseable using instructions on page 16 and sew the arms to the body at the shoulder.

CUFFS (MAKE 2):

The cuffs are crocheted separately and added to the arms, either at the wrist or at the elbow, where you have made a color change for the transition to the shirt.

Row 1: Beginning at the bottom edge of the cuff with A, ch 10, sc in 2nd ch from hook and next 8 ch—9 sts.

(If you are making cuffs to add to a child's shirt, fasten off after Row 1 and sew to arms.)

Row 2: Ch 1, turn, sc in each sc across.

Fasten off, leaving a long tail for sewing. Sew bottom edge of cuff to arm at color change, starting and ending at the outside of arm. Weave in ends.

BIKINI AND TANK TOP

Hey, ladies! Those female dolls who like a little more sun might want to wear the next top in the lineup. Either crochet a bikini top or extend the bodice as a tank top. You'll crochet the Curvy Top from the last pattern in the skin tone for your base, then begin the instructions below. The Child's Bikini and Tank Top follows the regular size and should be used with a Child's Basic Top crocheted in flesh-tone yarn.

Materials and Tools

- WORSTED-WEIGHT OR SPORT-WEIGHT YARN IN TOP COLOR (A) AND FLESH COLOR (B) OF YOUR CHOICE (REFER TO PAGE 12 FOR A LIST OF RECOMMENDED YARNS) (4)
- CROCHET HOOK: 3.5MM (SIZE E-4 U.S.)
- STITCH MARKER
- YARN NEEDLE
- POLYESTER FIBERFILL STUFFING
- NARROW WOODEN DOWEL, 6"/15CM LONG

Stitches and Techniques Used

- ADJUSTABLE RING, PAGE 20
- CHAIN (CH), PAGE 18
- SINGLE CROCHET (SC), PAGE 19
- SLIP STITCH (SL ST), PAGE 19
- HALF DOUBLE CROCHET (HDC), PAGE 21
- INVISIBLE DECREASE (INVDEC), PAGE 25
- BOBBLE (5 DC), PAGE 23

INSTRUCTIONS FOR aDULT

For a bikini or a tank top, you will first need to create the Curvy Top (page 52). Crochet the body and arms entirely in skin-tone yarn. Now that the body is made, the separate bikini top (or tank top) will be crocheted and sewn on. You will make the top "bra" pieces first and crochet them together. The bodice of the top will then be crocheted on.

Rnd 1: With A, make an adjustable ring, ch 1, work 6 sc into the ring. Pull closed—6 sts.

Rnd 2: Work 2 sc into each st around—12 sts.

Rnd 3: [2 sc into next st, sc into next 3 sts] 3 times—15 sts. Fasten off with a slip stitch into the next sc. Repeat these steps to make a second circle shape. Leave the yarn tail long on one of the circles. Lay the pieces next to each other and sew them together at one edge, to resemble a figure-eight shape for the bra.

Rnd 4: Draw up a loop of A on one end of the joined pieces, work 4 sc evenly spaced across the edge toward the middle, 3 hdc in the seam between circles, work 4 sc evenly spaced across to the opposite end of the joined pieces, ch 16, and join with a sl st to first st of this rnd (Rnd 4)—27 sts.

Rnd 5: Sl st into next 11 sts, sc into next 16 ch—27 sts.

If you are making a bikini top, fasten off here and weave in ends. Follow instructions below for sewing to the body. Continue on for crocheting a tank top.

Rnds 6–10: Hdc into each st around.

Fasten off with a slip stitch into the next sc and weave in ends.

FINISHING:

For contrast edging, draw up a loop of yarn (either B or another contrasting color) at the back of the top along the top edge and work one round of slip stitches all the way around. Weave in ends.

Fit top over body, pulling it up from the bottom. Position and use matching yarn to tack the top into place. Loop the yarn over the doll's shoulders tightly to create straps, coming up through the front of the top, over the shoulder, and back down into the back of the top, knotting tightly inside and snipping close to the surface.

INSTRUCTIONS FOR CHILD

To make the child's bikini or tank top, you need to first create the Child's Basic Top (page 45). Use a skin-tone yarn for the body and arms, or make a Child's Basic Top and put a tank top over it. You could even get creative and make the tank top the same color as one of the Skirt patterns (page 72) for a cute dress. Now that the body is made, the separate bikini top (or tank top) will be crocheted and sewn on. The top will be crocheted in one piece, short for a bikini top and longer for a tank. The top will be sewn onto the body of your doll, incorporating straps at the end.

Rnd 1: With A, ch 21, sl st into the first ch to form a ring; taking care not to twist ch, sc in each ch around (including same ch as joining sl st)—21 sts.

Rnds 2 and 3: Sc into each st around.

Rnd 4: Ch 2 (counts as hdc), skip next st, [hdc into next st, ch 1, skip next st] 10 times; join with sl st into top of beg ch-2—11 hdc and 10 ch-1 sps.

If making a bikini top, fasten off and weave in ends. Follow instructions for attaching it to body below.

Rnd 5: Ch 1, sc in first hdc (same st as joining sl st), sc into each hdc and ch-1 sp around. Do not join at the end of the rnd—21 sts.

Rnds 6 and 7: Sc into each st around.

Repeat Rnd 7 for a longer tank top.

Fasten off with a slip stitch into the next sc and weave in ends. Position top on the body under the arms. Join matching yarn with a slip stitch at the back of the top on one side. Ch 5 and join with slip stitch to front of top to complete a strap. Fasten off and weave in ends. Repeat on other side for second strap.

BLAZER

The first jacket is a blazer with lapels and buttons. Tiny snaps are sewn onto the inside to close the front. Sew on a felt pocket square for a debonair look! The blazer is created in three main pieces: the back and two front pieces. The sleeves and lapels are crocheted onto the assembled body of the blazer at the end. For the smaller Child's Blazer, follow the instructions to reduce the number of repeats within the pattern.

Materials and Tools

■ SPORT-WEIGHT YARN IN THE COLOR(S) OF YOUR CHOICE (A) (REFER TO PAGE 12 FOR A LIST OF RECOMMENDED YARNS) **(3)**

■ CROCHET HOOK: 3.5MM (SIZE E-4 U.S.)

■ STITCH MARKER

■ YARN NEEDLE

■ SEWING NEEDLE

■ MATCHING THREAD

■ 2 OR 3 BLACK OR SILVER SEW-ON METAL SNAPS, SIZE 3

■ 2 OR 3 SHANK BUTTONS, 3MM DIAMETER

Stitches and Techniques Used

■ CHAIN (CH), PAGE 18

■ SINGLE CROCHET (SC), PAGE 19

■ SLIP STITCH (SL ST), PAGE 19

■ DOUBLE CROCHET (DC), PAGE 22

■ HALF DOUBLE CROCHET (HDC), PAGE 21

■ HALF DOUBLE CROCHET TWO TOGETHER (HDC2TOG), PAGE 27

INSTRUCTIONS FOR ADULT

BACK:

Row 1: Starting at top of back of blazer, with A, ch 14, hdc into 3rd ch from hook and each ch across—12 sts.

Rows 2–12: Ch 2, turn, hdc into each st across—12 sts.

Repeat Row 2 for a longer blazer.

Fasten off and leave a long tail for sewing blazer together.

FRONT (MAKE 2):

Row 1: Starting at the top of the blazer and with A, ch 6, hdc into 3rd ch from hook and each ch across—4 sts.

Rows 2–4: Ch 2, turn, hdc into each st across—4 sts.

SHAPE ARMHOLE:

Row 5: Ch 4, turn, hdc into 3rd ch from hook and next ch, hdc into next 4 sts—6 sts.

SHAPE FRONT EDGE:

Row 6: Ch 2, turn, 2 hdc into next st, hdc into next 5 sts—7 sts.

Row 7: Ch 2, turn, hdc into each st across.

Row 8: Ch 2, turn, 2 hdc into first st, hdc into next 6 sts—8 sts.

Rows 9–12: Ch 2, turn, hdc into each st across—8 sts.

Repeat Row 9 for a longer blazer, being sure to have the same number of rows as the back of the blazer.

Fasten off and leave a long tail for sewing blazer together.

ASSEMBLY:

The long straight edge of each front is the outer/side edge. Place fronts on top of back, matching the side and top edges. Sew top edges of fronts to top edge of back for shoulder seams, leaving the center four stitches at the center top of the back unsewn. Sew the side edges together, beginning at the lower edge and sewing to the beginning of the armhole shaping. Leave the armhole unsewn. Sleeves will be crocheted directly into the armholes. Weave in ends.

SLEEVE (MAKE 2):

Rnd 1: Join A with sc at the shoulder seam and work 17 more sc evenly spaced around opening —18 sts.

Rnd 2: [Invdec, sc into next 4 sts] 3 times—15 sts.

Rnd 3: Hdc into next 7 sts, hdc2tog, hdc into next 6 sts—14 sts.

Rnd 4: Hdc into next 6 sts, hdc2tog, hdc into next 6 sts—13 sts.

Rnds 5 and 6: Hdc into each st around.

Rnd 7: Hdc into next 6 sts, hdc2tog, hdc into next 5 sts—12 sts.

Rnds 8 and 9: Hdc into each st around.

Rnds 10 and 11: Sc into each st around.

Fasten off with a slip stitch into the next sc. Weave in ends.

LAPELS:

You will start at the lower right front corner of the blazer (as worn) and work up the front edge, around the neck, and down the other front edge to the lower left front corner.

Note: If you lengthened the back and fronts of the blazer, you will need to add sc stitches to each side of the lapels.

Join yarn with sc at lower left front corner of blazer, sc in same place, working in ends of rows up front edge, work 2 sc in end of each of next 4 rows, (hdc, dc) in end of next row (corner at beginning of front neck shaping), 2 dc in end of next row, (dc, ch 3, sl st) in end of next row, (sl st, ch 3, dc) in end of next row, 2 dc in end of each of next 3 rows, dc in each st across back neck, 2 dc in end of each of next 3 rows, (dc, ch 3, sl st) in end of next row, (sl st, ch 3, dc) in end of next row, 2 dc in end of next row, (dc, hdc) in end of next row, 2 sc in end of each of last 5 rows.

Fasten off and weave in ends. With matching yarn, tack down corners of lapels to lie flat. Weave in ends.

INSTRUCTIONS FOR CHILD

The pattern for a child-size blazer follows the same formula as the Blazer and is made in the same way, with size adjustments to match the proportions of the child-size doll. The one shown here has been turned into a vest by omitting the sleeves.

CHILD'S BACK:

Row 1: Starting at top of jacket back with A, ch 12, hdc into 3rd ch from hook and each additional ch—10 sts.

Rows 2–9: Ch 2, turn, hdc into each st across—10 sts.

Fasten off and leave a long tail for sewing blazer together.

CHILD'S FRONT (MAKE 2):

Row 1: Starting at the top of the blazer with A, ch 5 hdc into 3rd chain from hook and each ch across—3 sts.

Rows 2 and 3: Ch 2, turn, hdc into each st across.

SHAPE ARMHOLES:

Row 4: Ch 4, turn, hdc into 3rd ch from hook and next ch, hdc into next 3 sts—5 sts.

SHAPE FRONT EDGE:

Row 5: Ch 2, turn, 2 hdc into next st, hdc into next 4 sts—6 sts.

Rows 6–9: Ch 2, turn, hdc into each st across.

Fasten off and leave a long tail for sewing blazer together.

ASSEMBLY:

The long straight edge of each front is the outer/side edge. Place fronts on top of back, matching the side and top edges. Sew top edges of fronts to top edge of back for shoulder seams, leaving the center four stitches at the center top of the back unsewn. Sew the side edges together, beginning at the lower edge and sewing to the beginning of the armhole shaping. Leave the armhole unsewn. Sleeves will be crocheted directly into the armholes. Weave in ends.

CHILD'S SLEEVE (MAKE 2):

Rnd 1: Join A with sc at the shoulder seam and work 14 more sc evenly spaced around opening —15 sts.

Rnd 2: Hdc2tog, hdc into next 13 sts—14 sts.

Rnd 3: Hdc into next 6 sts, hdc2tog, hdc into next 6 sts—13 sts.

Rnd 4: Hdc2tog, hdc into next 11 sts—12 sts.

Rnds 5–7: Sc into each st around—12 sts.

Fasten off with a slip stitch into the next sc. Weave in ends.

Going for a tough, rugged look? Turn any jacket pattern into a vest by leaving off the sleeves. A sleeveless windbreaker crocheted in soft cotton yarn makes a great denim vest.

CHILD'S LAPELS:

You will start at the lower left front corner of the blazer (as you're looking at it) and work up the front edge, around the neck, and down the other front edge to the lower right front corner. Join yarn with sc at lower left front corner of blazer, sc in same place, 2 sc in end of each of next 2 rows, (hdc, dc) in end of next row, (dc, ch 2, sl st) in end of next row, sc in end of next row, dc in each of next 2 rows, ch 2, hdc in end of next row.

This brings you to the back neckline of the jacket; hdc in each st across back neck. Working down other side of jacket, hdc in end of next row, ch 2, dc in end of next 2 rows, sc in end of next row, (sl st, ch 2, dc) in end of next row, (dc, hdc) in end of next row, 2 sc in end of each of last 3 rows.

Fasten off and weave in ends. With matching yarn, tack down corners of lapels to lie flat. Weave in ends.

FINISHING:

Sew snaps onto jacket following package directions using matching thread. Sew small shanked buttons onto outside of jacket (these are decorative only).

WINDBREAKER

The second option for a jacket is more of a windbreaker, with a boxy shape and a shorter length. The body of the jacket is worked in one piece, beginning at the neck edge. Openings are made for armholes, and sleeves are worked directly into these openings. Like the other jacket, this one can be made in sport-weight yarn for better drape. I've also included a pattern that makes an add-on hood, so you can turn this jacket into a hoodie in a few simple steps.

Materials and Tools

■ SPORT-WEIGHT YARN OR WORSTED WEIGHT IN THE COLOR(S) OF YOUR CHOICE (A) (REFER TO PAGE 12 FOR A LIST OF RECOMMENDED YARNS) **(3)** OR **(4)**

■ CROCHET HOOK: 3.5MM (SIZE E-4 U.S.)

■ STITCH MARKER

■ YARN NEEDLE

■ SEWING NEEDLE

■ MATCHING THREAD

■ 2 OR 3 BLACK OR SILVER SEW-ON METAL SNAPS, SIZE 3

Stitches and Techniques Used

■ CHAIN (CH), PAGE 18

■ SINGLE CROCHET (SC), PAGE 19

■ SLIP STITCH (SL ST), PAGE 19

■ DOUBLE CROCHET (DC), PAGE 22

■ DOUBLE CROCHET TWO TOGETHER (DC2TOG), PAGE 26

■ HALF DOUBLE CROCHET TWO TOGETHER (HDC2TOG), PAGE 27

INSTRUCTIONS FOR ADULT

With A, ch 21.

Row 1: Sc into 2nd ch from hook and next 19 ch—20 sts.

Row 2: Ch 3 (counts as first dc here and throughout), turn, dc into next 3 sts, 2 dc into each of next 2 sts, dc into next 8 sts, 2 dc into each of next 2 sts, dc into last 4 sts—24 sts.

Note: When a beginning ch-3 counts as a stitch, this means you should not work a dc into the first stitch of the previous row, and the last stitch of the next row should be worked into the top of the ch-3.

Row 3: Ch 3, turn, dc into next 4 sts, 2 dc into each of next 2 sts, dc into next 10 sts, 2 dc into each of next 2 sts, dc into next 5 sts—28 sts.

Row 4: Ch 3, turn, dc into next 4 sts, 2 dc into each of next 4 sts, dc into next 10 sts, 2 dc into each of next 4 sts, dc into next 5 sts—36 sts.

Row 5: Ch 3, turn, dc into next 5 sts, ch 6, skip next 6 sts (for armhole), dc into next 12 sts, ch 6, skip next 6 sts (for armhole), dc into next 6 sts—24 dc and 2 ch-6 sps.

Row 6: Ch 3, turn, dc into each st and ch across—36 sts.

Row 7: Ch 3, turn, dc into next 7 sts, dc2tog, dc into next 16 sts, dc2tog, dc into next 8 sts—34 sts.

Row 8: Ch 3, turn, dc into next 5 sts, dc2tog, dc into next 4 sts, dc2tog, dc into next 6 sts, dc2tog, dc into next 4 sts, dc2tog, dc into next 6 sts—30 sts.

Row 9: Ch 3, turn, dc into next 5 sts, dc2tog, dc into next 6 sts, dc2tog, dc into next 6 sts, dc2tog, dc into next 6 sts—27 sts.

Rows 10 and 11: Ch 1, turn, sc into each st across.

You will now work into the edge and collar of the jacket.

Row 12: Ch 1, turn to work across front edge of jacket, work 16 sc evenly spaced up front edge; working across opposite side of foundation ch at neck edge, (hdc, ch 2, dc, ch 2, hdc) into first ch (corner made), sc into next 18 ch across neck edge, (hdc, ch 2, dc, ch 2, hdc) into last ch (corner made), work 16 sc evenly spaced down other front edge—56 sts and 4 ch-2 sps.

Fasten off. Weave in ends.

SLEEVE (MAKE 2):

Rnd 1: Join A with a slip stitch at the back of the bottom of the armhole opening, ch 3 (counts as first dc here and throughout), work 15 dc evenly spaced around opening; join with a sl st to top of beg ch-3—16 sts.

Rnd 2: Ch 3, dc2tog, dc into next 6 sts, dc2tog, dc into next 5 sts; join with a sl st to top of beg ch-3—14 sts.

Rnd 3: Ch 3, dc into next 5 sts, dc2tog, dc into next 6 sts; join with a sl st to top of beg ch-3—13 sts.

Rnd 4: Ch 3, dc into next 8 sts, dc2tog, dc into next 2 sts; join with a sl st to top of beg ch-3—12 sts.

Rnd 5: Ch 1, invdec, sc into each st around; join with a sl st to top of beg ch-1—11 sts.

Rnd 6: Ch 1, sc into next 6 sts, invdec, sc into next 3 sts; join with a sl st to top of beg ch-1—10 sts.

Rnd 7: Ch 1, sc into each st around; join with a sl st to top of beg ch-1.

Fasten off with a slip stitch into the next sc and weave in ends.

Repeat for other sleeve.

FINISHING:

With matching thread, sew snaps onto jacket following package directions.

INSTRUCTIONS FOR CHILD

The windbreaker is made in the same way as the regular Windbreaker, with proportions matching the child-size doll.

CHILD'S BODY:

Row 1: With A, ch 15, sc into 2nd ch from hook and next 13 ch —14 sts.

Row 2: Ch 2, turn, 2 hdc into first, hdc into next 3 sts, 2 hdc into next st, hdc into next 4 sts, 2 hdc into next st, hdc into next 3 sts, 2 hdc last st—18 sts.

Row 3: Ch 2, turn, 2 hdc into first st, hdc into 3 sts, 2 hdc into next st, hdc into next 8 sts, 2 hdc into next st, hdc into next 3 sts, 2 hdc into last st—22 sts.

Row 4: Ch 2, turn, 2 hdc into first st, hdc into next 3 sts, ch 5, skip next 5 sts (for armhole), hdc into next 4 sts, ch 5, skip next 5 sts (for armhole), hdc into next 3 sts, 2 dc into last st—14 hdc and 2 ch-5 sps.

Row 5: Ch 2, turn, 2 hdc into first st, hdc into next 22 sts, 2 hdc in last st—26 sts.

Rows 6 and 7: Ch 2, turn, hdc into each st across.

Rows 8 and 9: Ch 1, turn, sc into each st across.

You will now work into the edge and collar of the jacket.

Row 10: Ch 1, turn to work across front edge of jacket, work 9 sc evenly spaced up front edge; working across opposite side of foundation ch at neck edge, 3 hdc into first ch (corner made), sc into next 12 ch across neck edge, 3 hdc into last ch (corner made), work 9 sc evenly spaced down other front edge—36 sts.

Fasten off. Weave in ends.

CHILD'S SLEEVE (MAKE 2):

Rnd 1: Join A with a slip stitch at the back of the bottom of the armhole opening, work 14 sc evenly spaced around opening; do not join rnds—14 sts.

Rnd 2: [Hdc2tog, hdc into next 5 sts] twice—12 sts.

Rnd 3: Hdc in each st around.

Rnds 4 and 5: Sc in each st around.

Rnd 6: Sc2tog, sc in next 10 sts —11 sts.

Rnds 7 and 8: Sc in each st around.

Fasten off with a slip stitch into the next sc and weave in ends.

FINISHING:

With matching thread, sew snaps onto jacket following package directions.

CARDIGAN

What's another item of clothing your doll might need? A cardigan, of course! This sweater is also best crocheted in sport-weight yarn so that it will have a more relaxed, draped fit. The adult size is worked from the top down, and similar to the Blazer (page 56), snaps are sewn in for closure and buttons are added on the outside for decoration. For the Child's Cardigan, you'll work from the bottom up.

Materials and Tools

- SPORT-WEIGHT YARN IN THE COLOR(S) OF YOUR CHOICE (A) (REFER TO PAGE 12 FOR A LIST OF RECOMMENDED YARNS) ③
- CROCHET HOOK: 3.5MM (SIZE E-4 U.S.)
- STITCH MARKER
- YARN NEEDLE
- SEWING NEEDLE
- MATCHING THREAD
- 2 OR 3 BLACK OR SILVER SEW-ON METAL SNAPS, SIZE 3
- 2 OR 3 BUTTONS, 3MM

Stitches and Techniques Used

- CHAIN (CH), PAGE 18
- SLIP STITCH (SL ST), PAGE 19
- SINGLE CROCHET (SC), PAGE 19
- HALF DOUBLE CROCHET (HDC), PAGE 21
- DOUBLE CROCHET (DC), PAGE 22
- DOUBLE CROCHET TWO TOGETHER (DC2TOG), PAGE 26
- HALF DOUBLE CROCHET TWO TOGETHER (HDC2TOG), PAGE 27

INSTRUCTIONS FOR aDULT

Row 1: Beginning at the top/neck edge with A, ch 15, work 2 sc into 2nd ch from hook, sc into next 12 ch, 2 sc into last ch—16 sts.

Row 2: Ch 3 (counts as first dc here and throughout), turn, dc into first st, dc into next 14 sts, 2 dc into last st—18 sts.

Row 3: Ch 3, turn, dc into next 2 sts, 2 dc into each next 2 sts, dc into next 8 sts, 2 dc into each of next 2 sts, dc into next 3 sts, working last dc into the top of the turning ch-3 from the previous row—22 sts.

Row 4: Ch 3, turn, dc into first st, dc into next 4 sts, 2 dc into each of next 2 sts, dc into next 8 sts, 2 dc into each next 2 sts, dc into next 4 sts, 2 dc into last st—28 sts.

Row 5: Ch 3, turn, dc into first st, dc into next 3 sts, ch 6, skip next 6 sts, dc into next 8 sts, ch 6, skip next 6 sts, dc into next 3 sts, 2 dc last st—18 sts and 2 ch-6 sps.

Row 6: Work into each dc and ch of previous row, ch 3, turn, dc into first st, 2 dc into each of next 2 sts, dc into next 4 sts, dc2tog, dc into next 12 sts, dc2tog, dc into next 4 sts, 2 dc into each of next 3 sts—34 sts.

Row 7: Ch 3, turn, skip first dc, dc into next 2 sts, dc2tog, dc into next 4 sts, dc2tog, dc into next 12 sts, dc2tog, dc into next 4 sts, dc2tog, dc into next 3 sts—30 sts.

Row 8: Ch 2, turn, hdc into each st across.

Row 9: Ch 2, turn, hdc into next 4 sts, hdc2tog, hdc into next 18, hdc2tog, hdc into next 4 sts—28 sts.

The next row is worked into the inside edge of the cardigan.

Row 10: Ch 1, turn to work across front edge of cardigan, work 15 sc evenly spaced across front edge.

Fasten off and weave in ends.

Row 11: Join A with a sl st at collar of right side of cardigan and work 15 sc evenly spaced down front edge. Fasten off and weave in ends.

SLEEVE (MAKE 2):

Sleeves are crocheted in rounds into the spaces made in Row 5. For ¾ sleeves, fasten off after Rnd 8.

Rnd 1: Join A with sc at back bottom edge of armhole opening, work 14 more sc evenly spaced around opening—15 sts.

Rnds 2–4: Hdc2tog, hdc into each st around—12 sts at end of Rnd 4.

Rnds 5–12: Sc into each st around.

Fasten off with a slip stitch in next sc and weave in ends.

FINISHING:

For a cardigan that can close, sew snaps to the inside with matching thread. Add buttons to the outside for decoration.

INSTRUCTIONS FOR CHILD

Row 1: Starting at the bottom of the cardigan with A, ch 22, hdc into 3rd ch from hook and next 19 ch—20 sts.

Rows 2–4: Ch 2, turn, hdc in each st around.

Row 5: Ch 2, turn, hdc2tog, hdc in

next 16 sts, hdc2tog—18 sts.

Row 6: Ch 2, turn, hdc2tog, hdc in next st, ch 5, skip next 3 sts, hdc in next 6 sts, ch 5, skip next 3 sts, hdc in next st, hdc2tog—10 hdc and 2 ch-5 sps.

Row 7: Work into each hdc and ch of previous row, ch 1, turn, sc2tog, sc in next 16 sts, sc2tog—18 sts.

Row 8: Ch 1, turn, sc2tog, sc in next 6 sts, sc2tog, sc in next 6 sts, sc2tog—15 sts.

Fasten off and weave in ends.

CHILD'S SLEEVE (MAKE 2):

Sleeves are crocheted in spiral rounds into the spaces made in Row 6 of the Cardigan. Complete the pattern as written for long sleeves. For three-quarter length sleeves, fasten off after Rnd 6.

Rnd 1: Join A with sc at back bottom edge of sleeve opening, work 12 more sc evenly spaced around opening—13 sts.

Rnd 2: Hdc into each st around.

Rnd 3: Hdc into next 4 sts, hdc2tog, hdc into next 7 sts—12 sts.

Rnd 4: Hdc2tog, hdc into next 10 sts—11 sts.

Rnds 5-8: Sc into each st around.

Fasten off with a slip stitch into the next sc and weave in ends. Repeat for other sleeve.

FINISHING:

Join A in lower front corner, sc evenly spaced up front edge, around neck, and down other front edge to opposite lower front corner.

With matching thread, sew snaps to inside of cardigan, and add buttons to the outside for decoration. Weave in any remaining ends.

LOWER BODY

At this point, your poor little creation has no lower body! Let's fix that. In the following section, you'll find options for different pants, shorts, and skirts, as well as options for giving your doll underwear and bare legs or tights. Will he have rocker skinny pants or would bootcut jeans suit him better? Should she wear a long flowy skirt over striped tights, or a sweet mini to show off her bare legs? You get to be your doll's own personal stylist! Make it work!

As you did with the upper body, you'll be choosing from various patterns to make your doll unique. Crochet the pants or legs first, then decide whether you want to add a skirt. There are two options for pants, one with a narrow leg opening and one with a flared leg opening. The first pants pattern can be shortened to create shorts or capri pants by simply changing color at different rows on the leg. You'll also find a pattern for bare legs with underwear and a pattern for legs with tights. The legs in these patterns get a little shaping and go great with one of the skirts, which you'll find next. Choose from a straight skirt or a full skirt with an optional trim. For a dress, match a skirt to the top you made in the previous chapter for a seamless look.

Again, as with the upper-body section, complete the patterns as written for an adult male or female doll, or follow the separate instructions for adjusting to the proportions of a child.

SKINNY PANTS

We'll start off with the most basic leg pattern. If you're making a male or female doll, the pattern will give you a skinny pant leg that is straight down and straightforward. Hipsters love these skinny pants. For child-size skinny pants, follow the separate pattern. Change to your flesh color anywhere along the leg to make shorts or capris. You'll start by crocheting the waist of the pants, continue down, and then split that section in half to form legs. After crocheting one leg all the way down, you will fasten off and rejoin your yarn where you split the pants before, and continue for the second leg. Sounds easy enough, right? If this is what your doll wants (and please don't forget to ask), let's begin!

Materials and Tools

■ WORSTED-WEIGHT YARN IN THE PANT COLOR(S) (A) AND OPTIONAL FLESH COLOR (B) OF YOUR CHOICE (REFER TO PAGE 12 FOR A LIST OF RECOMMENDED YARNS) **4**
■ CROCHET HOOK: 3.5MM (SIZE E-4 U.S.)
■ STITCH MARKER
■ YARN NEEDLE
■ POLYESTER FIBERFILL STUFFING

Stitches and Techniques Used

■ CHAIN (CH), PAGE 18
■ SINGLE CROCHET (SC), PAGE 19
■ INVISIBLE DECREASE (INVDEC), PAGE 25
■ SURFACE SLIP STITCH (SURFACE SL ST), PAGE 30

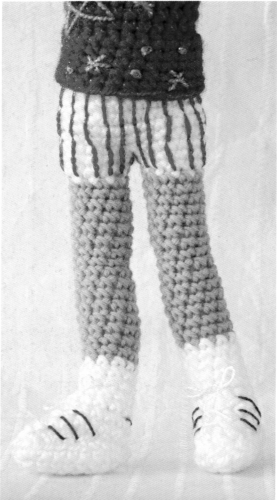

INSTRUCTIONS FOR aDULT

To shorten the pant length, change to B at the same row on both legs.

Rnd 1: Make a slip knot with A, leaving a 12"/30.5cm tail at the beginning. Ch 24; join with sl st in first ch to form a ring, taking care not to twist the chain. Sc into the next 23 ch around—24 sts.

Rnds 2–7: Sc into each st around.

FIRST LEG:

Rnd 8: Sc into first 12 sts, skip remaining 12 sts—12 sts.

This has split the pants in two, and you will now continue to crochet the first leg.

Rnd 9: Sc into first st of Rnd 8 and next 11 sts—12 sts.

Rnds 10–19: Sc into each st around.

Rnd 20: Invdec, sc into next 10 sts—11 sts.

Rnds 21–24: Sc into each st around.

Rnd 25: Invdec, sc into next 9 sts—10 sts.

Rnds 26–30: Sc into each st around.

Fasten off. Weave in ends.

SECOND LEG:

Rnd 8: Join yarn with sc in 13th st of Rnd 7 (first unworked st following First Leg), sc into next 11 sts—12 sts.

Rnd 9: Insert hook in corresponding st of First Leg and pull up a loop (2 loops on hook), insert hook in first st of Rnd 8 and pull up a loop, yarn over and draw through all 3 loops on hook, sc into next 11 sts.

Rnds 10–30: Repeat Rnds 10–30 of First Leg.

Fasten off. Weave in ends.

If you'd like to make a sewn-in belt, follow the instructions on page 106 for a surface slip-stitch belt, best made before you assemble the doll.

Using the long tail you started with, sew pants to the body of your doll at his or her waist. Weave in ends. Stuff the legs firmly.

INSTRUCTIONS FOR CHILD

To shorten the pant length, change to B at the same row on both legs.

Rnd 1: Make a slip knot with A, leaving a 12"/30.5cm tail at the beginning. Ch 20; join with sl st into first ch to form a ring, taking care not to twist the chain. Sc into the next 19 ch around—20 sts.

Rnds 2–5: Sc into each st around.

FIRST LEG:

Rnd 6: Sc into first 10 sts, skip remaining 10 sts—10 sts.

This has split the pants in two, and you will now continue to crochet the first leg.

Rnd 7: Sc into first st of Rnd 6 and next 9 sts—10 sts.

Rnd 8: Invdec, sc into next 8 sts —9 sts.

Rnds 9–12: Sc into each st around.

Rnd 13: Invdec, sc into next 7 sts— 8 sts.

Rnds 14–18: Sc into each st around.

Fasten off. Weave in ends.

SECOND LEG:

Rnd 6: Join yarn with sc into 11th st of Rnd 5 (first unworked st following First Leg), sc into next 9 sts— 10 sts.

Rnd 7: Insert hook in corresponding st of First Leg and pull up a loop (2 loops on hook), insert hook in first st of Rnd 6 and pull up a loop, yarn over and draw through all 3 loops on hook, sc into next 9 sts.

Rnds 8–18: Repeat Rnds 8–18 of First Leg.

Fasten off. Weave in ends.

If you'd like to make a sewn-in belt, follow the instructions on page 106 for a surface slip stitch belt.

Using the long tail you started with, sew pants to the body of your doll at his or her waist. Weave in ends. Stuff the legs firmly.

BOOTCUT PANTS

The second pattern for the legs of your doll is a teeny bit more complicated. It is strictly for long pants, and ends up with a bootcut fit at the bottom. There is a little trickery involved when you reach the calf area of the leg. You're going to work one row of the pants in the front loops only, which will give you a whole round on the inside of the pants to work into for the doll's leg. It will all make sense when you get there, so let's begin!

Materials and Tools

- WORSTED-WEIGHT YARN IN THE PANT COLOR(S) (A) AND FLESH COLOR OR SOCK COLOR (B) OF YOUR CHOICE (REFER TO PAGE 12 FOR A LIST OF RECOMMENDED YARNS) (4)
- CROCHET HOOK: 3.5MM (SIZE E-4 U.S.)
- STITCH MARKER
- YARN NEEDLE
- POLYESTER FIBERFILL STUFFING

Stitches and Techniques Used

- CHAIN (CH), PAGE 18
- SINGLE CROCHET (SC), PAGE 19
- FRONT LOOPS ONLY (FLO), PAGE 28
- INVISIBLE DECREASE (INVDEC), PAGE 25
- SURFACE SLIP STITCH (SURFACE SL ST), PAGE 30

INSTRUCTIONS FOR ADULT

Rnd 1: Make a slip knot with A, leaving a 12"/30.5cm tail at the beginning, ch 24; join with sl st into first ch to form a ring, taking care not to twist the chain. Sc into the next 23 ch around—24 sts.

Rnds 2–7: Sc into each st around.

FIRST LEG:

Rnd 8: Sc into first 12 sts, skip remaining 12 sts—12 sts.

This has split the pants in two, and you will now continue to crochet the first leg.

Rnd 9: Sc into first st of Rnd 8 and next 11 sts—12 sts.

Rnds 10–27: Sc into each st around.

Rnd 28: Sc into the FLO of each st around.

Rnd 29: Work 2 sc into next st, sc in next 11 sts—13 sts.

Rnd 30: Work 2 sc into next st, sc in next 12 sts—14 sts.

Fasten off. Weave in ends.

ANKLE BENEATH BELL OF PANT LEG:

Rnd 31: Fold pant leg along Rnd 28 to expose the unworked back loops of Rnd 27. Holding pants upside down, join B with sc at the back of the leg, and sc into next 11 sts—12 sts.

Rnd 32: [Invdec, sc into next 4 sts] twice—10 sts.

Rnd 33: Sc into each st around.

Fasten off. Weave in ends.

SECOND LEG:

Rnd 8: Join yarn with sc into 13th st of Rnd 7 (first unworked st following First Leg), sc into next 11 sts—12 sts.

Rnd 9: Insert hook in corresponding st of First Leg and pull up a loop (2 loops on hook), insert hook in first st of Rnd 8 and pull up a loop, yarn over and draw through all 3 loops on hook, sc into next 11 sts.

Rnds 10–33: Repeat Rnds 10–33 of First Leg.

Fasten off. Weave in ends.

INSTRUCTIONS FOR CHILD

Rnd 1: Make a slip knot with A, leaving a 12"/30.5cm tail at the beginning, ch 20; join with sl st into first ch to form a ring, taking care not to twist the chain. Sc into the next 19 ch around—20 sts.

Rnds 2–5: Sc into each st around.

FIRST LEG:

Rnd 6: Sc into first 10 sts, skip remaining 10 sts—10 sts.

This has split the pants in two, and you will now continue to crochet the first leg.

Rnd 7: Sc into first st of Rnd 6 and next 9 sts—10 sts.

Rnd 8: Invdec, sc into next 8 sts—9 sts.

Rnds 9–15: Sc into each st around.

Rnd 16: Sc into the FLO of each st around.

Rnd 17: Work 2 sc into next st, sc in next 8 sts—10 sts.

Rnd 18: Work 2 sc into next st, sc in next 9 sts—11 sts.

Rnd 19: Sc into each st around.

Fasten off. Weave in ends.

ANKLE BENEATH BELL OF PANT LEG:

Rnd 20: Fold pant leg along Rnd 16 to expose the unworked back loops of Rnd 15. Holding pants upside down, join B with sc at the back of the leg, and sc into next 8 sts—9 sts.

Rnd 21: Invdec, sc into next 7 sts—8 sts.

Rnds 22 and 23: Sc into each st around.

Fasten off. Weave in ends.

SECOND LEG:

Rnd 6: Join yarn with sc into 11th st of Rnd 5 (first unworked st following First Leg), sc into next 9 sts—10 sts.

Rnd 7: Insert hook in corresponding st of First Leg and pull up a loop (2 loops on hook), insert hook in first st of Rnd 6 and pull up a loop, yarn over and draw through all 3 loops on hook, sc into next 9 sts.

Rnds 8–23: Repeat Rnds 8–23 of First Leg.

If you'd like to make a sewn-in belt, follow the instructions on page 106 for a surface slip-stitch belt.

Using the long tail you started with, sew pants to the body of your doll at his or her waist. Weave in ends. Stuff the legs firmly.

BARE LEGS AND UNDERWEAR

The next lower-body pattern makes bare legs for your doll. We'll start with a color of your choice for the underwear portion of the pattern, then change to a flesh tone to make shapely legs. If you'd like to make your doll wearing socks, work the last couple of rounds in a sock color of your choice. The shoes will be created in the next section. This pattern can also be used to make shorts with shapely legs. Just complete the top part of the pattern in the shorts color of your choice without color changes. Change to a flesh color a few rows down the leg and continue with the pattern as written. This pattern is great along with one of the skirts, or alone as a bathing suit bottom. (Or maybe your doll just likes to walk around in his underwear all day. I won't judge.) Complete the regular pattern for an adult-size doll, or follow the separate instructions for a child-size doll.

Materials and Tools

- WORSTED-WEIGHT YARN IN THE UNDERWEAR COLOR (A) AND FLESH COLOR (B) OF YOUR CHOICE (REFER TO PAGE 12 FOR A LIST OF RECOMMENDED YARNS) (4)
- CROCHET HOOK: 3.5MM (SIZE E-4 U.S.)
- STITCH MARKER
- YARN NEEDLE
- POLYESTER FIBERFILL STUFFING

Stitches and Techniques Used

- CHAIN (CH), PAGE 18
- SINGLE CROCHET (SC), PAGE 19
- INVISIBLE DECREASE (INVDEC), PAGE 25

INSTRUCTIONS FOR aDULT

Rnd 1: Make a slip knot with A, leaving a 12"/30.5cm tail at the beginning, ch 24; join with sl st into first ch to form a ring, taking care not to twist the chain. Sc into the next 23 ch around—24 sts.

Rnd 2: Sc into each st around.

Rnd 3: With A, sc into next 4 sts, change to B, sc into next 4 sts, change to A, sc into next 8 sts, change to B, sc into next 4 sts, change to A, sc into next 4 sts.

Rnd 4: With A, sc into next 3 sts, change to B, sc into next 6 sts, change to A, sc into next 6 sts, change to B, sc into next 6 sts, change to A, sc into next 3 sts.

Rnd 5: With A, sc into next 2 sts, change to B, sc into next 8 sts, change to A, sc into next 4 sts, change to B, sc into next 8 sts, change to A, sc into next 2 sts.

Rnd 6: With A, sc into next st, change to B, sc into next 10 sts,

change to A, sc into next 2 sts, change to B, sc into next 10 sts, change to A, sc into next st.

FIRST LEG:

Rnd 7: Change to B in the last st of Rnd 6, sc into first 12 sts, skip remaining 12 sts—12 sts.

This has split the legs in two, and you will now continue to crochet the first leg.

Rnd 8: Sc into first st of Rnd 8 and next 11 sts—12 sts.

Rnd 9: Invdec, sc into each st around—11 sts.

Rnd 10: Sc into next 5 sts, invdec, sc into next 4 sts—10 sts.

Rnds 11–17: Sc in each sc around.

Rnd 18: Sc next 3 sts, invdec twice, sc in next 3 sc—8 sts.

Rnd 19: Sc next 3 sts, 2 sc in each of next 2 sc, sc in next 3 sc—10 sts.

Rnds 20–30: Sc in each sc around. Change to a contrasting color at the end of Rnd 26 for socks if desired.

Fasten off. Weave in ends.

SECOND LEG:

Rnd 7: Join B with sc in 13th st of Rnd 6 (first unworked st following First Leg), sc into next st and next 11 sts—12 sts.

Rnd 8: Insert hook in corresponding st of First Leg and pull up a loop (2 loops on hook), insert hook in first st of Rnd 7 and pull up a loop, yarn over and draw through all 3 loops on hook, sc in next 11 sts.

Rnds 9-7: Repeat Rnds 9–17 of First Leg—10 sts.

Rnd 18: Invdec, sc in next 6 sts, invdec—8 sts.

Rnd 19: Work 2 sc in next st, sc in next 6 sts, 2 sc in next st—10 sts.

Rnds 20–30: Sc in each sc around.

Change to a contrasting color at the end of Rnd 26 for socks if desired.

Fasten off. Weave in ends.

INSTRUCTIONS FOR CHILD

Rnd 1: Make a slip knot with A, leaving a 12"/30.5cm tail at the beginning, ch 20; join with sl st into first ch to form a ring, taking care not to twist the chain. Sc into the next 19 ch around—20 sts.

Rnd 2: Sc into each st around.

Rnd 3: With A, sc into next 3 sts, change to B, sc into next 5 sts, change to A, sc into next 5 sts, change to B, sc into next 5 sts, change to A, sc into next 2 sts.

Rnd 4: With A, sc into next 2 sts, change to B, sc into next 7 sts, change to A, sc into next 3 sts, change to B, sc into next 7 sts, change to A, sc into next st.

Rnd 5: With A, sc into next st, change to B, sc into next 9 sts, change to A, sc into next st, change to B, sc into next 9 sts, change to A, sc into next st.

FIRST LEG:

Rnd 6: Change to B in the last st of Rnd 5, sc into first 10 sts, skip remaining 10 sts—10 sts.

This has split the legs in two, and you will now continue to crochet the first leg.

Rnd 7: Sc into first st of Rnd 6 and next 9 sts—10 sts.

Rnd 8: Invdec, sc into each st around—9 sts.

Rnd 9: Sc into next 4 sts, invdec, sc into next 3 sts—8 sts.

Rnds 10 and 11: Sc in each sc around.

Rnd 12: Invdec twice, sc in next 4 sts—6 sts.

Rnd 13: Work 2 sc in each of next 2 sc, sc in next 4 sc—8 sts.

Rnds 14–17: Sc in each sc around.

Work Rnds 16 and 17 in a contrasting color for socks if desired.

Fasten off. Weave in ends.

SECOND LEG:

Rnd 6: Join B with sc in 11th st of Rnd 5 (first unworked st following First Leg), sc into next 9 sts—10 sts.

Rnd 7: Insert hook in corresponding st of First Leg and pull up a loop (2 loops on hook), insert hook in first st of Rnd 6 and pull up a loop, yarn over and draw through all 3 loops on hook, sc into next 9 sts.

Rnds 8–11: Repeat Rnds 8–11 of First Leg.

Rnd 12: Invdec, sc into next 4 sts, invdec—6 sts.

Rnd 13: Work 2 sc in next st, sc in next 4 sts, 2 sc in next st—8 sts.

Rnds 14–17: Sc in each sc around.

Work Rnds 16 and 17 in a contrasting color for socks if desired.

Using the long tail you started with, sew legs to the body of your doll at his or her waist. Weave in ends. Stuff the legs firmly.

TIGHTS

If you want to make a doll with a fashion-forward sense of style, crochet her some patterned tights. Houndstooth is trendy and achieved by changing color every round. The tiny "v's" of the stitches create the pattern. Stripes are created easily just by changing color every other round. Use a variegated yarn for an unpredictable, colorful pattern. A simple solid color might match her outfit better. You put together the look you want. These legs start in the color or pattern of your choice. They are also shaped at the calf to give them a "second-skin" look.

Materials and Tools
■ WORSTED-WEIGHT YARN IN THE TIGHTS COLOR (A) AND (B) OF YOUR CHOICE (REFER TO PAGE 12 FOR A LIST OF RECOMMENDED YARNS) **(4)**
■ CROCHET HOOK: 3.5MM (SIZE E-4 U.S.)
■ STITCH MARKER
■ YARN NEEDLE
■ POLYESTER FIBERFILL STUFFING

Stitches and Techniques Used
■ CHAIN (CH), PAGE 18
■ SINGLE CROCHET (SC), PAGE 19

INSTRUCTIONS FOR ADULT

Rnd 1: Make a slip knot with A, leaving a 12"/30.5cm tail at the beginning, ch 24; join with sl st into first ch to form a ring, taking care not to twist the chain. Sc into the next 23 ch around—24 sts.
For the remainder of the pattern, alternate colors between A and B as desired to create houndstooth (change every round), stripes (change every other round), or solid (use one color throughout). A single variegated yarn will make a random splotchy pattern throughout.
Rnds 2–6: Sc into each st around.

FIRST LEG:
Rnd 7: Sc into first 12 sts, skip remaining 12 sts—12 sts.
This has split the legs in two, and you will now continue to crochet the first leg.
Rnd 8: Sc into first st of Rnd 7 and next 11 sts—12 sts.
Rnd 9: Invdec, sc into each st around—11 sts.
Rnd 10: Sc into next 5 sts, invdec, sc into next 4 sts—10 sts.

Rnds 11–17: Sc in each sc around.
Rnd 18: Invdec twice, sc in next 6 sc—8 sts.
Rnd 19: Work 2 sc in each of next 2 sc, sc in next 6 sc—10 sts.
Rnds 20–30: Sc in each sc around. Fasten off. Weave in ends.

SECOND LEG:

Rnd 7: Join B with sc in 13th st of Rnd 6 (first unworked st following First Leg), sc into next 11 sts—12 sts.
Rnd 8: Insert hook in corresponding st of First Leg and pull up a loop (2 loops on hook), insert hook in first st of Rnd 7 and pull up a loop, yarn over and draw through all 3 loops on hook, sc into next 11 sts.
Rnds 9–11: Repeat Rnds 9–30 of First Leg.
Using the long tail you started with, sew legs to the body of your doll at his or her waist. Weave in ends. Stuff the legs firmly.

INSTRUCTIONS FOR CHILD

Rnd 1: Make a slip knot with A, leaving a 12"/30.5cm tail at the beginning, ch 20; join with sl st into first ch to form a ring, taking care not to twist the chain. Sc into the next 19 ch around—20 sts.
Rnds 2–5: Sc into each st around.

FIRST LEG:

Rnd 6: Sc into first 10 sts, skip remaining 10 sts—10 sts.
This has split the legs in two, and you will now continue to crochet the first leg.
Rnd 7: Sc into first st of Rnd 5 and next 9 sts—10 sts.
Rnd 8: Invdec, sc into each st around—9 sts.

Rnd 9: Sc into next 4 sts, invdec, sc into next 3 sts—8 sts.
Rnds 10 and 11: Sc in each sc around.
Rnd 12: Invdec twice, sc in next 4 sts—6 sts.
Rnd 13: Work 2 sc in each of next 2 sc, sc in next 4 sc—8 sts.
Rnds 14–17: Sc in each sc around. Fasten off. Weave in ends.

SECOND LEG:

Rnd 6: Join B with sc in 11th st of Rnd 5 (first unworked st following First Leg), sc into next 9 sts—10 sts.
Rnd 7: Insert hook in corresponding st of First Leg and pull up a loop (2 loops on hook), insert hook in first st of Rnd 6 and pull up a loop, yarn over and draw through all 3 loops on hook, sc into next 9 sts.
Rnds 8–11: Repeat Rnds 8–11 of First Leg.
Rnd 12: Invdec, sc into next 4 sts, invdec—6 sts.
Rnd 13: Work 2 sc in next st, sc in next 4 sts, 2 sc in next st—8 sts.
Rnds 14–17: Sc in each st around.
Using the long tail you started with, sew legs to the body of your doll at his or her waist. Weave in ends. Stuff the legs firmly.

STRAIGHT SKIRT

So you've decided to give your lady doll a skirt? The first option is for a straight skirt. It can't get any simpler than this pattern. You start with a foundation round and work as many additional rounds as needed for the length of skirt you want. Working with half double crochet stitches will make the finished fabric stretchy and soft. You may use worsted-weight yarn or sport-weight yarn for a lighter texture. Your doll may wear a super-short mini or a sleek pencil skirt, or crochet the skirt all the way down to her ankles as part of a formal ensemble. The finished skirt is sewn onto the body of the doll at the waist.

Materials and Tools

- WORSTED- OR SPORT-WEIGHT YARN IN THE COLOR OF YOUR CHOICE (A) (REFER TO PAGE 12 FOR A LIST OF RECOMMENDED YARNS) **(4)**
- CROCHET HOOK: 3.5MM (SIZE E-4 U.S.)
- STITCH MARKER
- YARN NEEDLE
- POLYESTER FIBERFILL STUFFING

Stitches and Techniques Used

- ADJUSTABLE RING, PAGE 20
- CHAIN (CH), PAGE 18
- SINGLE CROCHET (SC), PAGE 19
- HALF DOUBLE CROCHET (HDC), PAGE 21

INSTRUCTIONS FOR ADULT

Rnd 1: Make a slip knot with A, leaving a 12"/30.5cm tail at the beginning, ch 24; join with sl st into first ch to form a ring, taking care not to twist the chain. Sc into the next 23 ch around—24 sts.

Rnds 2–9: Hdc into each st around.

Repeat Rnd 9 until skirt is desired length.

Sc into first st of last rnd worked and sl st into the next st. This creates a smooth finish on the seam. Weave in ends.

Use the long tail you started with to sew the skirt to the body at the waist.

INSTRUCTIONS FOR CHILD

Rnd 1: Make a slip knot with A, leaving a 12"/30.5cm tail at the beginning, ch 21; join with sl st into first ch to form a ring, taking care not to twist the chain. Sc into the next 20 ch around—21 sts.

Rnds 2–5: Hdc into each st around.

Repeat Rnd 5 until skirt is desired length.

Sc into first st of last rnd worked and sl st into the next st. This creates a smooth finish on the seam. Weave in ends.

Use the long tail you started with to sew the skirt to the body at the waist.

FULL SKIRT

This skirt is fuller and crocheted in a lighter-weight yarn for better draping. You will use a double crochet stitch to achieve a softer fabric and flow. Instead of the spiral rounds you've been using, you will crochet in joined rounds. This skirt would be cute as part of a dress, matching the top's color, or as a separate. Crochet a scalloped edging for an extra-feminine touch. Better yet, use this pattern for a manly kilt!

Materials and Tools

- SPORT-WEIGHT YARN IN THE COLOR OF YOUR CHOICE (A) (REFER TO PAGE 12 FOR A LIST OF RECOMMENDED YARNS) (3)
- CROCHET HOOK: 3.5MM (SIZE E-4 U.S.)
- STITCH MARKER
- YARN NEEDLE
- POLYESTER FIBERFILL STUFFING

Stitches and Techniques Used

- ADJUSTABLE RING, PAGE 20
- CHAIN (CH), PAGE 18
- SINGLE CROCHET (SC), PAGE 19
- DOUBLE CROCHET (DC), PAGE 22

INSTRUCTIONS FOR aDULT

Rnd 1: Make a slip knot with A, leaving a 12"/30.5cm tail at the beginning, ch 25; join with sl st into first ch to form a ring, taking care not to twist the chain. Sc into the next 24 ch around—25 sts (including the joining sl st).

Rnd 2: Ch 3 (counts as dc here and throughout), dc into joining sl st, dc into each sc around; join with a sl st into top of beginning ch-3 (first dc)—26 dc.

Rnd 3: Ch 3, 2 dc into next st, dc into next 24 sts; join with a sl st into first dc—27 dc.

Rnd 4: Ch 3, [2 dc into next st, dc into next 12 sts] twice; join with a sl st into first dc—29 dc.

Rnd 5: Ch 3, [2 dc into next st, dc into next 13 sts] twice; join with a sl st into first dc—31 dc.

Rnd 6: Ch 3, [2 dc into next st, dc into next 14 sts] twice; join with a sl st into first dc—33 dc.

Rnd 7: Ch 3, [2 dc into next st, dc into next 15 sts] twice; join with a sl st into first dc—35 dc.

Rnd 8: Ch 3, [2 dc into next st, dc into next 16 sts] twice; join with a sl st into first dc—37 dc.

Rnd 9: Ch 3, 2 dc into next st, dc into each remaining st around; join with a sl st into first dc—38 dc.

Repeat Rnd 9 (increasing 1 st in each rnd) until skirt is desired length. Following the pattern, the skirt will continue to get wider and wider. If you'd prefer a slightly narrower skirt, do not include an increase in each rnd, but instead work even dc around. Continue with edging (optional) or fasten off and weave in ends.

PICOT EDGING:

Rnd 1: *(Sc, ch 2, sc) into next st, sc into next 2 sts; rep from * around, sc into any remaining sts; join with sl st into first sc. Fasten off and weave in yarn tail.

Use the long tail you started with to sew the skirt to the body at the waist.

INSTRUCTIONS FOR CHILD

Rnd 1: Make a slip knot with A, leaving a 12"/30.5cm tail at the beginning, ch 21; join with sl st into first ch to form a ring, taking care not to twist the chain. Sc into the next 20 ch around—21 sts (including the joining sl st).

Rnd 2: Ch 3 (counts as first dc here and throughout), dc in joining sl st, dc in next 5 sts, 2 dc in next st, [dc in next 6 sts, 2 dc in next st] twice; join with sl st into first dc (top of beginning ch-3)—25 sts.

Rnd 3: Ch 3, [dc in next 7 sts, 2 dc in next st] 3 times; join with sl st into first dc—28 sts.

Rnd 4: Ch 3, [dc in next 8 sts, 2 dc in next st] 3 times; join with sl st into first dc—31 sts.

Rnd 5: Ch 3, [dc in next 9 sts, 2 dc in next st] 3 times; join with sl st into first dc—34 sts.

Continue with optional edging in a contrasting color or fasten off and weave in ends.

PICOT EDGING:

Rnd 1: Join yarn with a sl st in any st, ch 1, (sc, ch 2, sc) into next st, *sc into next st, (sc, ch 2, sc) in next st; rep from * to end of rnd; join with sl st into beginning ch-1. Fasten off and weave in ends.

Use the long tail you started with to sew the skirt to the body at the waist.

FEET AND SHOES

Your amigurumi creation is starting to really take shape, isn't it? Before you can let him stand on his own two feet, though, you'll have to make him his own, uh, two feet. You can tell a lot about a person (in this case, a crocheted person) by his shoes, so give this part of your design special consideration.

The choice you make regarding shoes will determine a lot about the person. Maybe your doll is athletic, so make basic tennis shoes. If your doll is preppy, loafers are the way to go. Dressed up? Heels or wedges will be a good choice. Boots and hi-tops are crocheted over the doll's legs. For the ultimate in casual comfort, give your doll flip-flops. Your doll wears no shoes at all? I've even included a pattern for cute little bare feet.

Each of the following patterns is crocheted onto the bottoms of the legs that you just completed. Each pattern has instructions for crocheting adult-size feet as well as the child-size version.

BASIC FULL SHOE

The first shoe pattern is so basic that it can be pretty much any kind of shoe that covers the full foot. You can use white yarn and stitch stripes to the side to make sneakers, make a basic men's shoe using brown yarn, or crochet the tops and soles different colors. Add laces to complete the look. For low-top sneakers, work the shoe in one color through Round 2, and change to white yarn for the last round. A white sole finishes it off.

Materials and Tools

■ WORSTED-WEIGHT YARN IN THE SHOE COLOR(S) OF YOUR CHOICE (A) (REFER TO PAGE 12 FOR A LIST OF RECOMMENDED YARNS) **④**
■ CROCHET HOOK: 3.5MM (SIZE E-4 U.S.)
■ STITCH MARKER
■ YARN NEEDLE
■ POLYESTER FIBERFILL STUFFING

Stitches and Techniques Used

■ CHAIN (CH), PAGE 18
■ SINGLE CROCHET (SC), PAGE 19
■ SINGLE CROCHET TWO TOGETHER (SC2TOG), PAGE 24
■ DOUBLE CROCHET (DC), PAGE 22
■ HALF DOUBLE CROCHET (HDC), PAGE 21
■ SLIP STITCH (SL ST), PAGE 19

INSTRUCTIONS FOR aDULT

RIGHT SHOE:

Rnd 1: Make a slip knot with A, leaving a 6"/15cm tail at the beginning. Holding doll upside down and looking at the back of the legs, working around the last rnd of stitches in the right leg, join A with sc at one stitch to the left of the center back of the leg, sc into next 4 sc, 3 dc into next sc (for front of shoe), sc into next 4 sc—12 sts.

Rnd 2: Sc into next 6 sts, 3 dc into next st, sc into next 5 sts—14 sts.

Rnd 3: Sc into next 7 sts, 4 dc into next st, sc into next 6 sts—17 sts.

Fasten off, leaving a short tail. It will be tucked in after you create the Soles and assemble the feet.

LEFT SHOE:

Repeat Rnds 1–3 of Right Shoe, joining yarn at one stitch to the right of the center back of the leg. Fasten off and leave a short tail.

SOLE (MAKE 2):

Rnd 1: With A (or contrasting sole color), ch 7. Turn chain over and working into the bumps along the back of the chain, sc into 2nd ch from hook, sc into next 4 ch, 3 sc into last ch, turning to work into other side (top) of ch, sc in next 4 ch, 2 sc into starting ch—14 sts.

Rnd 2: Ch 1, sc into next 5 sts, 3 sc into next st, hdc into next st, 3 sc into next st, sc into next 6 sts; join with a sl st into beginning ch-1—18 sts.

Fasten off and leave a long tail for sewing to the shoe. Stuff shoe and bottom of leg firmly, and sew sole to shoe.

Repeat for sole of second shoe.

INSTRUCTIONS FOR CHILD

BASIC SHOE:

The pattern follows the regular Basic Full Shoe pattern but is adjusted proportionally for the smaller child-size doll.

Rnd 1: Make a slip knot with A, leaving a 6"/15cm tail at the beginning. Holding doll upside down and working around the last round of stitches in the right leg, join A with sc at one stitch to the left of the center back of the leg, sc into next 3 sc, 3 hdc into next sc, sc into next 3 sc—10 sts.

Rnd 2: Sc into next 5 sts, 3 hdc into next st (for front of shoe), sc into next 4 sts—12 sts.

Rnd 3: Sc into next 6 sts, (hdc, 2 dc, hdc) in next hdc, sc in next 5 sts—15 sts.

Rnd 4: Sc into each st around.

Fasten off, leaving a short tail. Repeat Rnds 1–4 for second leg, joining yarn at one stitch to the right of the center back of the leg.

CHILD'S SOLE (MAKE 2):

Row 1: With A, ch 3, sc into 2nd ch from hook and next ch—2 sts.

Row 2: Ch 1, turn, sc into each st across.

Row 3: Ch 1, turn, 2 sc into each st across—4 sts.

Row 4: Ch 1, turn, sc2tog twice—2 sts.

Rows 5 and 6: Ch 1, turn, sc into each st across.

Fasten off and leave a long tail for sewing to the shoe. Stuff shoe and bottom of leg firmly, and sew sole to shoe, positioning Row 1 at the toe of the shoe.

LACE 'EM UP

Shoelaces couldn't be easier to make for your doll. They're a quick add-on that give a lot of detail to those little feet. Start by threading a yarn needle with a long strand (18"/45.5cm) of yarn in the shoelace color of your choice. Knot the long end and thread into the bottom of the shoe through a hole in the stitches and up through a stitch, perforating the yarn. This keeps the knot from pulling through. Using straight stitches, stitch straight across, then come further up the shoe and stitch two "x's" going up the shoe. Near the ankle, come up again and form a loop, tie it off close to the surface, form another loop, tie it off close to the surface again, and pull the yarn back into the foot. Knot the yarn and thread it back into the shoe, clipping it close to the surface so it retracts back into the shoe.

LOAFERS

This pattern will make shoes with a more squared toe and an added tongue. This pattern also has a few rounds of visible socks, so choose your colors accordingly. Crochet these shoes in basic black for a slick loafer made for moonwalking. The rounds meant for socks can be made in a flesh tone and the shoes crocheted in brown to make adorable deck shoes.

Materials and Tools

■ WORSTED-WEIGHT YARN IN THE SOCK OR FLESH COLOR (A) AND SHOE COLOR(S) (B) OF YOUR CHOICE (REFER TO PAGE 12 FOR A LIST OF RECOMMENDED YARNS) **(4)**
■ CROCHET HOOK: 3.5MM (SIZE E-4 U.S.)
■ STITCH MARKER
■ YARN NEEDLE
■ POLYESTER FIBERFILL STUFFING

Stitches and Techniques Used

■ CHAIN (CH), PAGE 18
■ SINGLE CROCHET (SC), PAGE 19
■ DOUBLE CROCHET (DC), PAGE 22
■ FRONT LOOPS ONLY (FLO), PAGE 28
■ INVISIBLE DECREASE (INVDEC), PAGE 25

INSTRUCTIONS FOR ADULT

RIGHT LOAFER:

Rnd 1: Make a slip knot with A, leaving a 6"/15cm tail at the beginning. Holding doll upside down and working around the last round of stitches in the right leg, join A with sc at one stitch to the left of the center back of the leg, sc into next 9 sc—10 sts.

Rnd 2: Sc into next 4 sts, 3 dc into next st (for front of shoe), sc into next 4 sts, change to B in last st—12 sts.

Rnd 3: Sc into next 5 sts, (sc, ch 1) into FLO of next 3 sts, sc into next 4 sts—12 sc and 3 ch-1 sps.

Rnd 4: Sc into next 5 sts, working into unworked back loops of the next 3 sts from Rnd 3, sc into next st, 3 dc into next st, sc into next st, sc into next 4 sts—14 sts.

Rnd 5: Sc into next 7 sts, 3 dc into next st, sc into next 6 sts—16 sts.

Rnd 6: Sc into next 7 sts, (2 sc, 2

hdc) into next st, hdc into next st, (2 hdc, 2 sc) into next st, sc into next 6 sts—22 sts.

Fasten off, leaving a short tail. It will be tucked in after you create the soles and assemble the feet.

LEFT LOAFER:
Repeat Rnds 1–6 for Right Loafer, joining yarn at one stitch to the right of the center back of the leg. Fasten off and leave a short tail.

SOLE (MAKE 2):
With B, ch 4.
Row 1: Sc into 2nd ch from hook and next 2 ch—3 sts.
Rows 2 and 3: Ch 1, turn, sc into each st—3 sts.
Row 4: Ch 1, turn, sc into next st, 2 sc into next st, sc into next st—4 sts.
Rows 5–7: Ch 1, turn, sc into each st across.

Fasten off and leave a long tail for sewing to the shoe. Stuff shoe and bottom of leg firmly, and sew sole to shoe.

Repeat for sole of second shoe.

INSTRUCTIONS FOR CHILD
LOAFER:
The Child's Loafer pattern follows the regular Loafer pattern but is adjusted proportionally for the smaller child-size doll.
Rnd 1: Make a slip knot with A (sock or flesh color), leaving a 6"/15cm tail at the beginning. Holding doll upside down and working around the last round of stitches in the right leg, join A with sc at one stitch to the left of the center back of the leg, sc into next

3 sc, 3 sc into next sc, sc into next 3 sc, change to B in last st—10 sts.
Rnd 2: Sc into next 4 sts, (sc, ch 1) into FLO of next 3 sts, sc into next 3 sts—10 sc and 3 ch-1 sps.
Rnd 3: Sc into next 4 sts, working into unused back loops of next 3 sts, sc into next st, 3 hdc into next st, sc into next st, sc in next 3 sts—12 sts.
Rnd 4: Sc into next 6 sts, 3 hdc into next st, sc into next 5 sts—14 sts.
Rnd 5: Sc into next 6 sts, (2 sc, 2 hdc) into next st, hdc into next st, (2 hdc, 2 sc) into next st, sc into next 5 sts—20 sts.

Fasten off, cutting tail short. Repeat Rnds 1–5 for second leg, joining yarn at one stitch to the right of the center back of the leg.

CHILD'S SOLE (MAKE 2):
With A, ch 3.
Row 1: Sc into 2nd ch from hook and next ch—2 sts.
Row 2: Ch 1, turn, sc into each st across.
Row 3: Ch 1, turn, 2 sc into first st, sc into next st—3 sts.
Row 4: Ch 1, turn, sc in each st across.
Row 5: Ch 1, turn, 2 sc into first st, sc into next 2 sts—4 sts.
Row 6: Ch 1, turn, sc in each st across.
Row 7: Ch 1, turn, sc in first st, invdec, sc in next st—3 sts.

Fasten off and leave a long tail for sewing to the shoe. Stuff shoe and bottom of leg firmly, and sew sole to shoe, positioning Row 1 at the toe of the shoe.

Repeat for sole of second shoe.

HIGH HEELS/FLATS

All dressed up or just going for an ultra-feminine look? High heels flatter real women, so your doll will probably appreciate the extra centimeter or two she'll get from these crocheted versions. You'll start with a skin-toned yarn (or yarn the color of tights, if applicable) and work down the foot, changing to a shoe color for the rest of the foot. The heel is worked into the back of the shoe and a sole is crocheted separately and sewn on.

I've included instructions to turn these shoes into flats. Follow the directions within the pattern to leave off the heel. Add a strap across the foot with a simple chain for Mary Janes!

Materials and Tools

- WORSTED-WEIGHT YARN IN THE FLESH OR TIGHTS COLOR (A) AND SHOE COLOR(S) (B) OF YOUR CHOICE (REFER TO PAGE 12 FOR A LIST OF RECOMMENDED YARNS) **(4)**
- CROCHET HOOK: 3.5MM (SIZE E-4 U.S.)
- STITCH MARKER
- YARN NEEDLE
- POLYESTER FIBERFILL STUFFING

Stitches and Techniques Used

- CHAIN (CH), PAGE 18
- SINGLE CROCHET (SC), PAGE 19
- SINGLE CROCHET TWO TOGETHER (SC2TOG), PAGE 24
- HALF DOUBLE CROCHET (HDC), PAGE 21

INSTRUCTIONS FOR aDULT

HIGH HEELS/FLATS:

Rnd 1: Make a slip knot with A, leaving a 6"/15cm tail at the beginning. Holding doll upside down and working around the last round of stitches in the right leg, join A with sc at one stitch to the left of the center back of the leg, sc into next 4 sc, 3 hdc into next sc, sc into next 4 sc—12 sts.

Rnd 2: Sc into next 6 sts, 3 hdc into next st, sc into next 5 sts—14 sts.

Rnd 3: Change to B at the end of Rnd 2. Sc into next 7 sts, (hdc, 2 dc, hdc) in next hdc, sc in next 6 sts—17 sts.

Rnd 4: Sc into each st around.

If you're making flats, fasten off at the end of Rnd 4.

In the next three rows, you will begin working in short rows to create a flat piece coming off the back of the shoe. It will be folded and stitched together to create the high heel.

Row 5: Sc into next 3 sts; leave remaining sts unworked.

Row 6: Ch 1, turn, sc into next 4 sts.

Row 7: Ch 1, turn, sc into next 4 sts.

Row 8: Ch 1, turn, skip first 3 sc and sl st into last sc, folding Rows 5–7 in half to create the heel.

Fasten off, leaving a long tail. Use the yarn tail to sew up to Row 5, closing heel.

Repeat Rnds 1–4 and Rows 5–8 for second leg, joining yarn at one stitch to the right of the center back of the leg.

SOLE (MAKE 2):

With B, ch 3.

Row 1: Sc into 2nd ch from hook and next ch—2 sts.

Row 2: Ch 1, turn, sc into each st across.

Row 3: Ch 1, turn, 2 sc into each st across—4 sts.

Row 4: Ch 1, turn, sc2tog twice —2 sts.

Row 5: Ch 1, turn, sc into each st across.

If you are making flats, repeat Row 5 two more times.

Fasten off and leave a long tail for sewing to the shoe. Stuff shoe and bottom of leg firmly, and sew sole to shoe in front of the heel.

Repeat for sole of second shoe.

INSTRUCTIONS FOR CHILD
HIGH HEELS/FLATS:

Rnd 1: Make a slip knot with A, leaving a 6"/15cm tail at the beginning. Holding doll upside down and working around the last round of stitches in the right leg, join

A with sc at one stitch to the left of the center back of the leg, sc into next 3 sc, 3 hdc into next sc, sc into next 3 sc—10 sts.

Rnd 2: Sc into next 5 sts, 3 hdc into next st, sc into next 4 sts, change to B in last st—12 sts.

Rnd 3: Sc into next 6 sts, (hdc, 2 dc, hdc) in next hdc, sc in next 5 sts—15 sts.

Rnd 4: Sc into each st around.

In the next three rows, you will begin working in short rows to create a flat piece coming off the back of the shoe. It will be folded and stitched together to create the high heel. If you're making flats, fasten off at the end of Rnd 4.

Row 5: Sc into next 2 sts; leave remaining sts unworked.

Row 6: Ch 1, turn, sc into next 4 sts.

Row 7: Ch 1, turn, sc into next 4 sts.

Row 8: Ch 1, turn, skip first 3 sc and sl st into last sc, folding Rows 5–7 in half to create the heel.

Fasten off, leaving a long tail. Use the yarn tail to sew up to Row 5, closing heel.

Repeat Rnds 1–4 and Rows 5–8 for second leg, joining yarn at one stitch to the right of the center back of the leg.

CHILD'S SOLE (MAKE 2):

With B, ch 3.

Row 1: Sc into 2nd ch from hook and next ch—2 sts.

Row 2: Ch 1, turn, sc into each st across.

Row 3: Ch 1, turn, 2 sc into each st across—4 sts.

Row 4: Ch 1, turn, sc2tog twice— 2 sts.

Row 5: Ch 1, turn, sc into each st across.

If you are making flats, repeat Row 5.

Fasten off and leave a long tail for sewing to the shoe. Stuff shoe and bottom of leg firmly, and sew sole to shoe in front of the heel.

Repeat for sole of second shoe.

Mary Janes:

After assembling the shoes, create a strap by joining yarn at one side of the shoe with a slip stitch, chain 4, and join on the other side of the shoe with a slip stitch. Cut yarn and weave in ends, pulling tails on either end of the chain strap into the shoe. Repeat for other shoe.

WEDGE HEELS

Slightly more casual than a traditional high heel, wedge heels will give your doll a lift with a mod look. The open toe of the wedge heels in the pattern below will look great with a summer dress or capri pants. The heel and toe strap can both be crocheted in the same color, or make the heel portion and toe strap different colors for a color-blocked look.

Materials and Tools

■ WORSTED-WEIGHT YARN IN THE FLESH OR TIGHTS COLOR (A) AND SHOE COLOR(S) (B) OF YOUR CHOICE (REFER TO PAGE 12 FOR A LIST OF RECOMMENDED YARNS) ④
■ CROCHET HOOK: 3.5MM (SIZE E-4 U.S.)
■ STITCH MARKER
■ YARN NEEDLE
■ POLYESTER FIBERFILL STUFFING

Stitches and Techniques Used

■ CHAIN (CH), PAGE 18
■ SINGLE CROCHET (SC), PAGE 19
■ SINGLE CROCHET TWO TOGETHER (SC2TOG), PAGE 24
■ HALF DOUBLE CROCHET (HDC), PAGE 21
■ DOUBLE CROCHET (DC), PAGE 22

INSTRUCTIONS FOR ADULT

WEDGE HEELS:

Rnd 1: Make a slip knot with A, leaving a 6"/15cm tail at the beginning. Holding doll upside down and working around the last round of stitches in the right leg, join with sc at one stitch left of the center back of the leg, sc into next 3 sc, (hdc, dc, hdc) into next sc, sc into next 5 sc, change to B in last st—12 sts.

Rnd 2: Sc into next 3 sts, change to A, sc into next 2 sts, (hdc, dc, hdc) into next st, sc into next 2 sts, change to B, sc into next 4 sts—14 sts.

Rnd 3: Sc into next 4 sts, change to A, sc into next 2 sts, (hdc, 2 dc, hdc) into next st, sc into next 2 sts, change to B, sc into next 5 sts—17 sts.

Rnd 4: Sc into next 4 sts, change to A, sc into next 3 sts, 2 hdc into each of next 2 sts, sc into next 2 sts, change to B, sc into next 6 sts—19 sts.

Row 5: Sl st into next 4 sts, sc into next 4 sts; leave remaining sts unworked—4 sts.

STRAP:

Rows 6–12: Ch 1, turn, sc into next 2 sts—2 sts.

Fasten off, leaving a 6"/15cm tail. Fold strap created in Rows 6–12 over the top of the foot and sew into place on the other side with the yarn tail.

Repeat Rnds/Rows 1–12 for second foot, joining yarn at one stitch to the right of the center of the back of the leg.

SOLE (MAKE 2):

With B, ch 4.

Row 1: Sc in 2nd ch from hook and next 2 ch—3 sts.

Rows 2–5: Ch 1, turn, sc in each sc across.

Row 6: Ch 1, turn, sc in first sc, 2 hdc in next sc, sc in last sc—4 sts.

Fasten off, leaving a long tail for sewing. Stuff shoe and bottom of leg firmly, and sew sole to shoe. Repeat for sole of second shoe.

INSTRUCTIONS FOR CHILD

WEDGE HEELS:

Rnd 1: Make a slip knot with A, leaving a 6"/15cm tail at the beginning. Holding doll upside down and working around the last round of stitches in the right leg, join A with sc at one stitch left of the center back of the leg, sc into next 2 sc, (hdc, dc, hdc) into next sc, sc into next 4 sc, change to B in last st—10 sts.

Rnd 2: Sc into next 2 sts, change to A, sc into next 2 sts, (hdc, dc, hdc) into next st, sc into next 2 sts, change to B, sc into next 3 sts—12 sts.

Rnd 3: Sc into next 3 sts, change to A, sc into next 2 sts, (hdc, 2 dc, hdc) into next st, sc into next 2 sts, change to B, sc into next 4 sts—15 sts.

Rnd 4: Sl st into next 3 sts, sc into next 2 sts; leave remaining sts unworked—2 sts.

STRAP:

Rows 5–10: Ch 1, turn, sc into next 2 sts—2 sts.

Fasten off, leaving a 6"/15cm tail. Fold strap created in Rows 5–10 over the top of the foot and sew into place on the other side with the yarn tail.

Repeat Rnds/Rows 1–10 for second foot, joining yarn at one stitch to the right of the center of the back of the leg.

CHILD'S SOLE (MAKE 2):

With B, ch 3.

Row 1: Sc into 2nd ch from hook and next ch—2 sts.

Row 2: Ch 1, turn, sc into each st across.

Row 3: Ch 1, turn, 2 sc into each st—4 sts.

Row 4: Ch 1, turn, sc2tog twice—2 sts.

Rows 5 and 6: Ch 1, turn, sc into each st across.

Fasten off and leave a long tail for sewing to the shoe. Stuff shoe and bottom of leg firmly, and sew sole to shoe. Repeat for sole of second shoe.

HI-TOPS AND BOOTS

Nothing says hipster cool like a pair of old-school hi-tops. If your doll is more in touch with her country roots, crochet some boots. They are basically the same, differing only in the addition of shoelaces and color choices. For boots, try a basic brown or black with a black sole. Work boots get added shoelaces. For hi-tops, choose a bright color for the shoes, changing to white on the last row. Crochet the sole in white to complete the look. Stitch shoelaces (page 78) all the way up.

For a hi-top or boot, you'll complete the pattern for a Basic Full Shoe, crochet it all the way through, then flip it over and crochet the top of the shoe up along the leg. This pattern may be used with the Bootcut Pants pattern, but keep in mind that because both have a free-hanging portion apart from the leg, they won't overlap smoothly and will have a bulkier look.

Materials and Tools

- WORSTED-WEIGHT YARN IN THE SHOE COLOR(S) OF YOUR CHOICE (A) (REFER TO PAGE 12 FOR A LIST OF RECOMMENDED YARNS) **(4)**
- CROCHET HOOK: 3.5MM (SIZE E-4 U.S.)
- STITCH MARKER
- YARN NEEDLE
- POLYESTER FIBERFILL STUFFING

Stitches and Techniques Used

- CHAIN (CH), PAGE 18
- SINGLE CROCHET (SC), PAGE 19
- SINGLE CROCHET TWO TOGETHER (SC2TOG), PAGE 24
- DOUBLE CROCHET (DC), PAGE 22
- BACK LOOPS ONLY (BLO), PAGE 28

INSTRUCTIONS FOR aDULT

HI-TOP/BOOT:

Rnd 1: Make a slip knot with A, leaving a 6"/15cm tail at the beginning. Holding doll upside down and working into the last round of stitches in the right leg, join A with sc at one stitch to the left of the center back of the leg. Work one row of sc around the leg. After crocheting the round of sc, work a round of sl st all the way around. This will be where you crochet into for the top portion of the hi-top or boot.

Rnd 2: Working into Rnd 1 (not the row of sl sts), sc into next 5 sc, 3 dc into next sc, sc into next 4 sc —12 sts.

Rnd 3: Sc into next 6 sts, 3 dc into next st, sc into next 5 sts—14 sts.

For an old-school hi-top sneaker, change to a contrasting color for Rnd 4.

Rnd 4: Sc into next 7 sts, 4 dc into next st, sc into next 6 sts—17 sts.

Fasten off, leaving a short tail. It will be tucked in after you create the soles and assemble the feet.

Repeat Rnds 1–4 for second leg, joining yarn at one stitch to the right of the center back of the leg. Fasten off and leave a short tail.

TOP OF SHOE:

Rnd 1: Holding doll upright and facing away from you, join yarn with sc in the back of the round of sl st you created along the top of the shoe, 2 sc into BLO of next sl st, sc in BLO of each sl st around —11 sts.

Rnds 2–4: Sc in next 11 sts— 11 sts.

Repeat Rnd 2 for higher boots or hi-tops if desired. Sl st into next st and fasten off. Weave in ends. Repeat for second shoe.

SOLE (MAKE 2):

Rnd 1: With A (or contrasting sole color), ch 7. Turn chain over and working into the bumps along the back of the chain, sc into 2nd ch from hook, sc into next 4 ch, 3 sc into last ch, turning to work into other side (top) of ch, sc into next 4 ch, 2 sc into starting ch—14 sts.

Rnd 2: Ch 1, sc into next 5 sts, 3 sc into next st, hdc into next st, 3 sc into next st, sc into next 6 sts; join with sl st into beginning ch-1— 18 sts.

Fasten off and leave a long tail for sewing to the shoe. Stuff shoe and bottom of leg firmly, and sew sole to shoe.

Repeat for sole of second shoe.

INSTRUCTIONS FOR CHILD

HI-TOP/BOOT:

Rnd 1: Make a slip knot with A, leaving a 6"/15cm tail at the beginning. Holding doll upside down and working into the last round of stitches in the right leg, join A with sc at one stitch to the left of the center back of the leg. Work one round of sc around the leg. After crocheting the round of sc, work a round of sl st all the way around. This will be where you crochet into for the top portion of the hi-top or boot.

Rnd 2: Sc into next 3 sts, 3 hdc into next st, sc into next 4 sts—10 sts.

Rnd 3: Sc into next 4 sts, 3 hdc in next hdc, sc in next 5 sts—12 sts.

For hi-tops, change color at the end of Rnd 4.

Rnd 4: Sc into next 5 sts, 4 hdc in next hdc, sc in next 6 sts—15 sts.

Fasten off, cutting tail short. Repeat Rnds 1–4 for second leg, joining yarn at one stitch to the right of the center back of the leg.

CHILD'S TOP OF SHOE:

Rnd 1: Holding doll upright and facing away from you, join yarn with a sc in the back of the row of sl st you created along the top of the shoe, 2 sc into BLO of next st, sc in BLO of each st around—9 sts.

Rnds 2 and 3: Sc in next 9 sts— 9 sts.

Repeat Rnd 2 for higher boots or hi-tops if desired. Sl st into next st and fasten off. Weave in ends. Repeat for second shoe.

CHILD'S SOLE (MAKE 2):

With B, ch 3.

Row 1: Sc into 2nd ch from hook and next ch—2 sts.

Rows 2 and 3: Ch 1, turn, sc into each st across.

Row 4: Ch 1, turn, 2 sc into each st across—4 sts.

Row 5: Ch 1, turn, sc2tog twice— 2 sts.

Row 6: Ch 1, turn, sc into each st across.

Fasten off and leave a long tail for sewing to the shoe. Stuff shoe and bottom of leg firmly, and sew sole to shoe.

Repeat for sole of second shoe.

FLIP-FLOPS

If you live somewhere with warm weather, chances are you have at least a couple of pairs of flip-flops. I won't tell you how many pairs I own, but I will tell you that they definitely are my favorite kind of shoe! Each pair gets worn 'til they fall apart, that's for sure. Crochet bare feet for your doll, then you'll make a flip-flop sole and strap in any color or colors you want. Any doll will be comfortable in a pair of flip-flops!

Materials and Tools

■ WORSTED-WEIGHT YARN IN THE FLESH COLOR (A) AND SHOE COLOR(S) (B) OF YOUR CHOICE (REFER TO PAGE 12 FOR A LIST OF RECOMMENDED YARNS) **4**
■ CROCHET HOOK: 3.5MM (SIZE E-4 U.S.)
■ STITCH MARKER
■ YARN NEEDLE
■ POLYESTER FIBERFILL STUFFING

Stitches and Techniques Used

■ CHAIN (CH), PAGE 18
■ SINGLE CROCHET (SC), PAGE 19
■ HALF DOUBLE CROCHET (HDC), PAGE 21
■ DOUBLE CROCHET (DC), PAGE 22
■ BOBBLE [2 DC], PAGE 23

INSTRUCTIONS FOR aDULT

FLIP-FLOPS:

Rnd 1: Make a slip knot with A, leaving a 6"/15cm tail at the beginning. Holding doll upside down and working around the last round of stitches in the right leg, join A with sc at one stitch to the left of the center back of the leg, sc again in same st as joining, sc in next 3 sts, 2 hdc in each of next 2 sts, sc in next 3 sts, 2 sc in next st—14 sts.

Rnd 2: Sc into next 7 sts, hdc into next st, 2 hdc into next st, hdc into next st; leave remaining sts unworked—11 sts.

Row 3: Ch 2, turn, hdc into next 4 sts; leave remaining sts unworked—4 sts.

Row 4: Ch 2, turn, (make Bobble, sl st) into each of next 4 sts.

Row 5: Do not turn, rotate piece to work across side edge of foot, sl st at beginning of side edge, work 5 sc evenly spaced down side edge—5 sc and 1 sl st.

Fasten off, leaving a long tail. Using a yarn needle, weave tail through next 5 stitches in the back of the leg and pull to cinch heel together. Knot tail on the inside and cut short. Repeat Rnds/Rows 1–5 for the second leg, joining yarn at one stitch to the right of the center back of the leg.

SOLE (MAKE 2):

Rnd 1: With B, ch 7. Turn chain over and working into the bumps along the back of the chain, sc into 2nd ch from hook, sc into next 4 ch, 3 sc into last ch, turning to work into other side (top) of ch, sc in next 4 ch, 2 sc into starting ch—14 sts.

Rnd 2: Ch 1, sc into next 4 sts, 3 sc into next st, 2 hdc into each of next 3 sts, 3 sc into next st, sc into next 5 sts; join with a sl st into beginning ch-1—21 sts.

Rnd 3: Ch 1, sc into each sc around.

Fasten off and leave a long tail for sewing to the foot. Stuff foot and bottom of leg firmly, and sew sole to foot, being careful to hide your stitches by inserting the needle into the back loop only of each stitch on the foot.

Repeat for sole of second foot.

STRAP:

With B, ch 10. Fasten off and leave a long tail for sewing. Stitch one end of the chain to top of foot starting at one side, stitch center of chain between the first and second toes, and stitch the other end of the chain to the other side of the shoe. Hide yarn ends inside the foot. Repeat for other shoe.

INSTRUCTIONS FOR CHILD

FLIP-FLOPS:

Rnd 1: Make a slip knot with A, leaving a 6"/15cm tail at the beginning. Holding doll upside down and working around the last round of stitches in the right leg, join A with sc at one stitch to the left of the center back of the leg, sc again in same st, sc in next 2 sts, 2 hdc in each of next 2 sts, sc in next 2 sts, 2 sc in next st—12 sts.

Rnd 2: Sc into next 6 sts, 2 sc into next st, sc into next st; leave remaining sts unworked—9 sts.

Row 3: Ch 1, turn, sc into next 4 sts; leave remaining sts unworked—4 sts.

Row 4: Ch 2, turn, (make Bobble, sl st) into each of next 4 sts—4 sts.

Row 5: Do not turn, rotate piece to work across side edge of foot, sl st at beginning of side edge, work 5 sc evenly spaced down side edge—5 sts and 1 sl st.

Fasten off, leaving a long tail. Using a yarn needle, weave tail through next 3 stitches in the back of the leg and pull to cinch heel together. Knot tail on the inside and cut short. Repeat Rnds/Rows 1–5 for the second leg, joining yarn at one stitch to the right of the center back of the leg.

CHILD'S SOLE (MAKE 2):

Rnd 1: With B, ch 5. Turn chain over and working into the bumps along the back of the chain, sc into 2nd ch from hook, sc into next 2 ch, 3 sc into last ch, turning to work into other side (top) of ch, sc in next 2 ch, 2 sc into starting ch—10 sts.

Rnd 2: Ch 1, sc into next 2 sts, 3 sc into next st, 2 hdc into each of next 3 sts, 3 sc into next st, sc into next 3 sts, sl st into next st—17 sts.

Rnd 3: Ch 1, sc into each sc around.

Fasten off and leave a long tail for sewing to the foot. Stuff shoe and bottom of leg firmly, and sew sole to foot, being careful to hide your stitches by inserting the needle into the back loop only of each stitch on the foot.

Repeat for sole of second foot.

CHILD'S STRAP:

With B, ch 8. Fasten off and leave a long tail for sewing. Stitch one end of the chain to top of foot starting at one side, stitch center of chain between the first and second toes, and stitch the other end of the chain to the other side of the shoe. Hide yarn ends inside the foot. Repeat for other shoe.

BARE FEET

Bare feet on your doll instantly give the look of a free spirit. They're a necessity if your doll is a hippie!

Materials and Tools

■ WORSTED-WEIGHT YARN IN THE FLESH COLOR OF YOUR CHOICE (A) (REFER TO PAGE 12 FOR A LIST OF RECOMMENDED YARNS) **④**
■ CROCHET HOOK: 3.5MM (SIZE E-4 U.S.)
■ STITCH MARKER
■ YARN NEEDLE
■ POLYESTER FIBERFILL STUFFING

Stitches and Techniques Used

■ CHAIN (CH), PAGE 18
■ SINGLE CROCHET (SC), PAGE 19
■ HALF DOUBLE CROCHET (HDC), PAGE 21
■ DOUBLE CROCHET (DC), PAGE 22
■ BOBBLE [3 DC], PAGE 23

INSTRUCTIONS FOR aDULT

BARE FEET:

Rnd 1: Make a slip knot with A, leaving a 6"/15cm tail at the beginning. Holding doll upside down and working around the last round of stitches in the right leg, join A with sc at one stitch to the left of the center back of the leg, sc again in same st, sc in next 3 sts, 2 hdc in each of next 2 sts, sc in next 3 sts, 2 sc in next st—14 sts.

Rnd 2: Sc into next 7 sts, hdc into next st, 2 hdc into next st, hdc into next st; leave remaining sts unworked—11 sts.

Row 3: Ch 2, turn, hdc into next 4 sts; leave remaining sts unworked—4 sts.

Row 4: Ch 2, turn, (make Bobble, sl st) into next 4 sts—4 sts.

Row 5: Do not turn, rotate piece to work across side edge of foot, sl st at beginning of side edge, work 6 sc evenly spaced down side edge—6 sts and 1 sl st.

SOLE:

Rows 6–8: Ch 1, turn, sc into next 6 sc—6 sts.

Row 9: Ch 1, rotate piece to work in short edge of sole of foot, hdc in end of next row, 2 hdc in end of next row, hdc end of next row—4 sts.

Fasten off, leaving a long tail. Stuff the foot firmly. Use the yarn tail to sew Rows 6–9 to the other side of the foot, being sure to sew closed the heel area and the area behind the toes.

Repeat Rnds/Rows 1–9 for second leg, joining yarn at one stitch to the right of the center back of the leg.

INSTRUCTIONS FOR CHILD

BARE FEET:

Rnd 1: Make a slip knot with A, leaving a 6"/15cm tail at the beginning. Holding doll upside down and working around the last round of stitches in the right leg, join A with sc at one stitch to the left of the center back of the leg, sc again in same st, sc in next 2 sts, 2 hdc in each of next 2 sts, sc in next 2 sts, 2 sc in next st—12 sts.

Rnd 2: Sc into next 6 sts, 2 sc into next st, sc into next st; leave remaining sts unworked—9 sts.

Row 3: Ch 1, turn, sc into next 4 sts; leave remaining sts unworked—4 sts.

Row 4: Ch 2, turn, (make Bobble, sl st) into next 4 sts—4 sts.

Rnd 5: Do not turn, sl st into side of foot, sc into next 5 sts down the side of the foot and around to the back of the leg—5 sts.

CHILD'S SOLE:

Rows 6–8: Ch 1, turn, sc into next 5 sc—5 sts.

Row 9: Ch 1, rotate piece to work in short edge of sole of foot, hdc in end of next row, 2 hdc in end of next row, hdc end of next row—4 sts.

Fasten off, leaving a long tail. Stuff the foot firmly. Use the yarn tail to sew Rows 6–9 to the other side of the foot, being sure to sew closed the heel area and the area behind the toes.

Repeat Rnds/Rows 1–9 for second leg, joining yarn at one stitch to the right of the center back of the leg.

HAIR

Consider your own hairstyle. Do you keep it long and natural? Is your hair short and low-maintenance? Did you dye it a wild color to stand out? Maybe you're working that Afro. From a long braid to a spiky mohawk, most hairstyles are an outward expression of identity. Keep this in mind when you're making your doll's hair. The color and texture of the yarn you choose will make a big impact on the look. It can be easily manipulated to look pretty much however you want. I'll show you several types of yarns and which hair textures can be achieved with each one.

Most of the hair patterns start with a wig cap, a cap that you'll crochet in the hair color of your choice and sew onto your doll's head. Wig caps are very easy to make. They follow the doll's head pattern. For example, if you are making a female doll with the Long and Narrow Female Head pattern, you would crochet the wig cap following that head pattern from the top, down several rows. The same formula, explained thoroughly below, applies to a child's and a male's wig cap. The actual strands of hair will then be embroidered or hooked into this wig cap. After creating the wig cap and hooking the hair into it, you'll cut and style it. You don't even need a cosmetology license—I promise!

Beyond hairstyles, I've also included instructions for creating facial hair. Make a mustache, goatee, or beard for your doll. Make it neat and groomed, or long and scruffy.

CHOOSING YARN

Once you start looking, you'll probably be surprised at how many interesting options are out there for making hair out of yarn! Sure, the standard worsted-weight varieties make nice straight hair in many different colors, but check out that novelty yarn aisle! All of the yarns I've listed below are only suggestions. Yarn companies are always coming up with new textures and fun novelty yarns, so be on the lookout for fun ones to add to your stash!

WORSTED-WEIGHT YARN

Available in arguably the greatest number of colors, good old worsted-weight yarn makes great doll hair as it is, albeit thick and straight. Use a few strands of slightly lighter colored yarn mixed in with your main color for highlights.

Roving-style yarn is yarn that has no twist and is single ply. It's readily available in worsted weight and makes excellent dreadlocks!

Separating the twist in plied yarn will create beautiful curly textured hair. With the dull pointed end of a yarn needle, separate the plies starting at the "root" of the hair (the place where it is hooked into the yarn cap) and gently "rake" through to the ends. The resulting hair will be fluffy and wavy.

FINE-GAUGE YARN

Using a lighter weight yarn will give your doll's hair a natural softness and looseness that you won't get from a standard worsted weight. Make sure you use enough strands. The finer gauge will give you less coverage over the wig caps and the hair will appear thin if you're not careful.

BOUCLE

If you look at a strand of boucle yarn, you'll see a variety of thicknesses, loops, and curls. Boucle yarn makes a great African-American hair texture and usually drapes beautifully. It gives the appearance of tight curls.

BULKY/FUR/CHENILLE

Fluffier types of yarn can all be classified in the same section. Their uses range from making soft, thick, long hair to making a mohawk. Some of these bulky yarns, after being crocheted, can be brushed gently with a bristled brush or dog slicker brush to create an even fuzzier texture. This should be tested out first. The brushed fabric hides stitch definition and works perfectly for a short beard or an Afro.

WIG CAPS

If you think of the doll's hair as a wig, you'll be creating the cap first, which fits over the head tightly. Because I give you a variety of head patterns, the wig cap you crochet will be based on the head you choose. Wig caps should be made with a worsted- or bulky-weight yarn. Although the doll's hair may be a novelty yarn or a finer weight, the cap should be sturdy and matching in gauge to the crocheted head. If you're using a bulky-weight yarn for the wig cap, make sure you "try on" the wig cap so as not to make it too big. You may need to leave out a row of increases to accommodate the bulk of the yarn. Match the color of the cap as closely as possible to the hair. When you sew on the wig cap, insert stuffing at the front of the head for height and volume if you'd like. A pompadour requires it!

After creating the wig cap, continue on to the next section and choose a hairstyle. If your doll has a short haircut, you will complete the hairstyle in this step when you sew on the wig cap. If your doll is going to have a mohawk or if you're leaving his or her head bald, you can skip this section!

male

LONG AND NARROW MALE HEAD (PAGE 33)

Follow the instructions for the head through Rnd 11 in your wig cap color of choice. For a widow's peak, hdc into next st, dc into next st, 2 dc into next st, dc into next st, hdc into next st, sc into next st, sl st into next st. Fasten off and leave a very long tail (20"/51cm). Position the wig cap tilted back on the head. Please note that the stitches in the cap and head should not line up. Use the yarn tail to stitch the cap to the head along the edge, using longer stitches for sideburns and/or a widow's peak along the top center of the hairline.

SHORT AND WIDE MALE HEAD (PAGE 34)

Follow the pattern for the head through Rnd 11 in your wig cap color of choice. For a widow's peak, hdc into next st, dc into next st, 2 dc into next st, dc into next st, hdc into next st, sc into next st, sl st into next st. Fasten off and leave a very long tail (20"/51cm). Position the wig cap tilted back on the head. Take note that the stitches in the cap and the stitches in the head should not line up. Use the yarn tail to stitch the cap to the head along the edge, using longer stitches for sideburns and/or a widow's peak along the top center of the hairline.

female

LONG AND NARROW FEMALE HEAD (PAGE 35)

Crochet the wig cap following the pattern for the head through Rnd 10, using your wig cap color of choice. For a widow's peak, hdc into next st, dc into next st, 2 dc into next st, dc into next st, hdc into next st, sc into next st, sl st into next st. Fasten off and leave a very long tail (20"/51cm). Position the wig cap tilted back on the head. The stitches in the head and the stitches in the cap should not line up. Use the yarn tail to stitch the cap to the head along the edge. If the female doll will have a short haircut, use the yarn tail to add sideburns around the ears.

SHORT AND WIDE FEMALE HEAD (PAGE 37)

Follow the pattern for the head through Rnd 10, using your wig cap color of choice. For a widow's peak, hdc into next st, dc into next st, 2 dc into next st, dc into next st, hdc into next st, sc into next st, sl st into next st. Fasten off and leave a very long tail (20"/51cm). Position the wig cap tilted back on the head. The stitches in the head and those in the cap should not line up. Use the yarn tail to stitch the cap to the head along the edge, using longer stitches around the sides of the cap for sideburns, if necessary.

CHILD
BASIC CHILD'S HEAD (PAGE 38)

Follow the pattern for the head through Rnd 8 in your wig cap color of choice. Fasten off and leave a long tail (12"/30.5cm). Position the wig cap tilted back on the head. Take note that the stitches in the cap and the stitches in the head should not line up. Use the yarn tail to stitch the cap to the head along the edge, using longer stitches for sideburns and/or a widow's peak along the top center of the hairline.

WIDE AND ROUND CHILD'S HEAD (PAGE 39)

Crochet the wig cap following the pattern for the head through Rnd 8, using your wig cap color of choice. Fasten off and leave a long tail (12"/30.5cm). Position the wig cap tilted back on the head. The stitches in the head and the stitches in the cap should not line up. Use the yarn tail to stitch the cap to the head along the edge, making longer stitches around the sides of the cap for sideburns, if necessary.

SHORT HAIR

For a short haircut, male or female, use matching yarn to add any straight stitches on the wig cap for more dimension. It's up to you. Add just a few stitches in the front and around the back, or stitch all over the wig cap for a solid covering of "hair." A little stuffing added under the wig cap will give lift to the front of your doll's hair if you'd like a pompadour or just more volume.

LONG HAIR

After you've created the wig cap, and you've decided your doll will have long hair, get to work putting the actual strands of hair in place. You can use any of the aforementioned yarns for this step.

Depending on the length you want your hair to be, you're going to cut strands of yarn. I like to do this first so that I can work through a big pile of strands quickly, hooking them into place. Whatever length you want the hair to be, you'll want to double that and add a few inches. It is better to err on the side of making the strands too long. If the strands are too short, you won't get the look you're going for in the end. For example, if you want the doll's hair to be pretty long, say, 5"/12.5cm down her back, you would want to cut strands of yarn at least 12"/30.5cm long.

Begin at the front hairline, starting at the point next to an ear, and work across the forehead and back down to the other ear. Insert a crochet hook into the front loop of a stitch, hook the middle of a strand, and pull up a loop. Wrap the ends of the strand around the hook and pull them through the loop. The motion is similar to the technique used in latch hooking. The strand is secure. Continue across the front and around the sides and back of the head. Once the hairline is filled in, choose where you want the part to be (middle or side). Like you did along the hairline, "latch hook" a row of

strands down each side of the imaginary part, stopping at the crown of the head. Hook a perpendicular row of strands across the back of the head that intersects with the rows along the part. Repeat another line of strands a few rows down. If you feel the wig cap needs to be filled in, repeat the process, trying to work in even, straight rows.

After the wig cap is sufficiently dense with hair, you can style the hair. Leave it straight and simple, or for wavy or curly hair, follow instructions on page 97. Trim the hair to the desired length. For a bob, cut it to the shoulder. Stitch the strands along the front hairline off to the side for side-swept bangs. Simply thread a yarn needle with the strand itself and insert the needle through a stitch in the wig cap. Pull it through and repeat as desired for strands around the front.

For a bob that curls under, leave strands long. Separate the hair into four even sections around the head and gather each section into a very loose ponytail. Tie with a scrap of matching yarn. Trim each section to be about ½"/1.5cm longer than where you tied the ponytails. Bring each side section back, the left under the left middle section, the right under the right middle section, and fold under. Use the yarn tail from the ponytail to sew into place. Now cover the ends with the middle sections, folding them down and over the side sections. Fold the ends of these middle sections under and use the yarn tails from tying the ponytails to sew them into place. Trim any hanging ends and tuck them under and in with a crochet hook, if necessary.

Long hair on your doll, just like on a real person, can be styled in many different ways:

• Use a scrap of yarn and tie the hair back into a ponytail.
• Separate the hair into sections and make one or more braids.
• For a formal updo, twist the whole bunch of hair in one piece, fold the ends under, and stitch in place with matching yarn. Have fun! Fixing these long hairstyles is one of my favorite parts of making dolls!

SURFACE CURLS

If your doll is blessed with natural curls, there's a way to make them out of yarn. They are fully customizable. Make tight curls as bangs or go all out and make dozens of long curls all over your doll's head. First you'll need to make a wig cap for your doll and sew it into place. Each curl is crocheted into the cap in rows. Start at the outside and work your way in toward the center of the head. Use sport- or worsted-weight yarn. Bulky yarn will make the curls less defined.

Materials and Tools

- SPORT- OR WORSTED-WEIGHT YARN IN THE HAIR COLOR OF YOUR CHOICE (REFER TO PAGE 12 FOR A LIST OF RECOMMENDED YARNS) **3** OR **4**
- CROCHET HOOK: 3.5MM (SIZE E-4 U.S.)
- STITCH MARKER
- YARN NEEDLE
- MATCHING EMBROIDERY FLOSS
- POLYESTER FIBERFILL STUFFING

Stitches and Techniques Used

- SLIP STITCH (SL ST), PAGE 19
- CHAIN (CH), PAGE 18
- SINGLE CROCHET (SC), PAGE 19

INSTRUCTIONS

Row 1: Join yarn with a sl st into a stitch on cap. Ch 5–21 sts. (Fewer chains will produce shorter curls; longer chains will produce very long curls.) Work 2 sc into the 2nd ch from hook and each ch across. The chain will curl on its own. Sl st into original st and next st. Repeat, working curling chains into every other stitch in the desired area, or all over the cap. Fasten off and weave in ends.

AFRO

When nothing but an Afro will do, you're in luck because this is one of the simplest hairstyles to make. It's so easy, yet so effective, and always recognizable and fun. Remember, no wig cap is necessary for this hairstyle. Because bulky yarn is sometimes difficult to sew with (especially into the tight stitches of your doll's head), I recommend using a matching embroidery floss to attach the Afro to the head. Follow the separate instructions for crocheting a child-sized Afro.

Materials and Tools
- BULKY- OR SUPER-BULKY WEIGHT YARN IN THE HAIR COLOR OF YOUR CHOICE (REFER TO PAGE 12 FOR A LIST OF RECOMMENDED YARNS) **(5)** OR **(6)**
- CROCHET HOOK: 4.0MM (SIZE G-6 U.S.)
- STITCH MARKER
- YARN NEEDLE
- MATCHING EMBROIDERY FLOSS
- POLYESTER FIBERFILL STUFFING

Stitches and Techniques Used
- ADJUSTABLE RING, PAGE 20
- CHAIN (CH), PAGE 18
- SINGLE CROCHET (SC), PAGE 19
- SINGLE CROCHET 2 TOGETHER (SC2TOG), PAGE 24
- HALF DOUBLE CROCHET (HDC), PAGE 25
- INVISIBLE DECREASE (INVDEC), PAGE 25

INSTRUCTIONS FOR aDULT

Rnd 1: Starting at crown of cap, make an adjustable ring, ch 1, work 6 sc into the ring. Pull closed—6 sts.

Rnds 2 and 3: Work 2 sc into each st around—24 sts at end of Rnd 3.

Rnd 4: *2 sc into next st, sc into next 3 sts; rep from * to end of rnd—30 sts.

Rnd 5: *2 sc into next st, sc into next 4 sts; rep from * to end of rnd—36 sts.

Rnd 6: Sc into each st around.

Rnd 7: *Sc2tog, sc into next 4 sts; rep from * rep to end of rnd—30 sts.

Rnds 8 and 9: Sc into each st around.

Row 10: Ch 1, turn, sc2tog, sc into next 2 sts, hdc into next 3 sts, sc into next 2 sts, sc2tog; leave remaining sts unworked—9 sts.

Row 11: Ch 1, turn, sc2tog, sc into next st, hdc into next 3 sts, sc into next st, sc2tog—7 sts.

Fasten off, leaving a short tail. Position wig cap on head with Rows 10 and 11 in front. If your doll has a high forehead or receding hairline, position Rows 10 and 11 in the back of the head. Stitch to head with the embroidery floss, stuffing evenly.

For a fuller Afro, use a short-bristled brush or dog slicker brush to brush the surface of the hair in all directions. The yarn will become fuzzy and stitches will become less noticeable.

INSTRUCTIONS FOR CHILD

Rnd 1: Starting at crown of cap, make an adjustable ring, ch 1, work 6 sc into the ring. Pull closed—6 sts.

Rnd 2: Work 2 sc into each st around—12 sts.

Rnd 3: *2 sc into next st, sc into next st; rep from * to end of rnd—18 sts.

Rnd 4: *2 sc into next st, sc into next 2 sts; rep from * to end of rnd—24 sts.

Rnd 5: *Invdec, sc into next 2 sts; rep from * to end of rnd—18 sts.

Rnd 5: Sc into each st around.

Fasten off and use the yarn tail or matching yarn to sew the Afro to the doll, stuffing as you go. Make a few tiny stitches with the yarn tail to make a natural-looking hairline. Weave in ends.

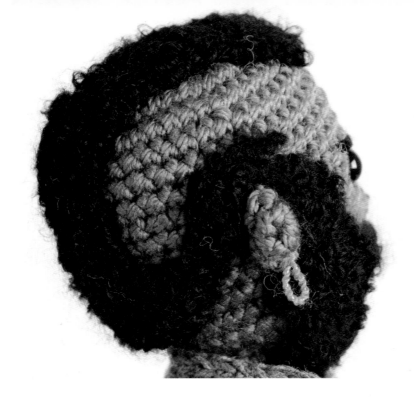

MOHAWK

Forget the conventional—if your doll wants to live on the edge, he needs a mohawk! You can use basic brown or black yarn, but crocheting this do in a wild, sparkly color would be an awesome look! Fur yarn held together with matching worsted yarn makes it easy. Crochet a strip of hair and sew it down. Instant punk!

INSTRUCTIONS FOR aDULT

Row 1: Using a combination of worsted weight and fur/eyelash yarn held together (or one color bulky weight yarn of your choice), ch 4, sc into 2nd ch from hook and next 2 ch—3 sts.

Rows 2–15: Ch 1, sc into each sc across.

Fasten off and leave a long tail for sewing. Sew the mohawk to the head down the middle, stuffing slightly if desired. Weave in ends.

Add several straight stitches along the side of the head if you'd like the mohawk to connect to the sideburns.

INSTRUCTIONS FOR CHILD

Row 1: Work as above.

Rows 2–10: Work as above.

Fasten off and leave a long tail for sewing. Sew the mohawk to the head down the middle, stuffing slightly if desired. Weave in ends.

Add several straight stitches along the side of the head if you'd like the mohawk to connect to the sideburns.

Materials and Tools

■ WORSTED-WEIGHT YARN IN THE HAIR COLOR OF YOUR CHOICE (REFER TO PAGE 12 FOR A LIST OF RECOMMENDED YARNS) (4)

■ COORDINATING FUR OR EYELASH YARN (5) OR BULKY OR SUPER-BULKY YARN (5) OR (6)

■ CROCHET HOOK: 4.0MM (SIZE G-6 U.S.)

■ YARN NEEDLE

Stitches and Techniques Used

■ ADJUSTABLE RING, PAGE 20

■ CHAIN (CH), PAGE 18

■ SINGLE CROCHET (SC), PAGE 19

BEAUTIFULLY BALD

If you're making a bald doll, you may still want a few strands of hair. Follow instructions for attaching the strands to a wig cap (page 94), attaching the strands directly to the doll's bald head. Sometimes the strands look funny on their own, but you can experiment with different lengths or add a complementary cap (see page 92).

FACIAL HAIR

Hipsters everywhere are sporting this classic look. Go for a thick '70s soup strainer or a sleek '40s pencil mustache. Crochet it long down the sides of the mouth for a biker-style horseshoe mustache. Whichever style you choose, a mustache makes a statement. Depending on the look you want, use a weight of yarn that matches the doll's hair. Go a step further to make a goatee or soul patch. Simply stitch under the chin with matching yarn, as directed below.

INSTRUCTIONS

For a very thin mustache, thread a yarn needle with the yarn of your choice and embroider a mustache on the doll's face using straight stitches. Make sure the stitches go into the actual stitches in the doll's head, not between stitches, so that they look even and stay in place. Weave in ends. Goatee or soul patch? Use the same yarn to add some straight stitches to your doll's chin.

For other types of mustaches, follow the instructions below. For a longer mustache, make the foundation chain longer. For a shorter mustache, make it shorter.
Row 1: Ch 11, sc into 2nd ch from hook and next 9 ch—10 sts.

For a thick mustache, ch 1, turn, and work another row of sc into Row 1.

Fasten off, leaving a long tail. Position the mustache onto the face with the center just below the doll's nose. Sew into place with the yarn tail or matching embroidery floss.

Materials and Tools

■ SPORT-, WORSTED-, OR BULKY-WEIGHT YARN MATCHING YOUR DOLL'S HAIR (REFER TO PAGE 12 FOR A LIST OF RECOMMENDED YARNS) **④** OR **⑤**
■ CROCHET HOOK: 4.0MM (SIZE G-6 U.S.) OR LARGER IF NECESSARY
■ YARN NEEDLE

Stitches and Techniques Used

■ CHAIN (CH), PAGE 18
■ SINGLE CROCHET (SC), PAGE 19

BEARD

A man with a beard has an air of masculinity about him, right? Make your doll's beard thick and long with fuzzy yarn or neat and tidy with worsted- or finer-weight yarn.

Materials and Tools

■ SPORT-WEIGHT, WORSTED-WEIGHT, OR BULKY YARN MATCHING YOUR DOLL'S HAIR (REFER TO PAGE 12 FOR A LIST OF RECOMMENDED YARNS) (3), (4), OR (5)

■ CROCHET HOOK: 4.0MM (SIZE G-6 U.S.) OR LARGER IF NECESSARY

■ YARN NEEDLE

Stitches and Techniques Used

■ CHAIN (CH), PAGE 18

■ SINGLE CROCHET (SC), PAGE 19

■ HALF DOUBLE CROCHET (HDC), PAGE 21

INSTRUCTIONS

Row 1: Ch 15, sc into 2nd ch from hook and next 3 ch, ch 6, sk next 6 ch, sc into next 4 ch—14 sts.

Row 2: Ch 1, turn, sc2tog, sc into next 2 sts, sc into next 6 ch, sc into next 2 sts, sc2tog—12 sts.

Row 3: Ch 1, turn, sc2tog, sc into next st, hdc into next 6 sts, sc into next st, sc2tog—10 sts.

Row 4: Ch 1, turn, sc into each st across.

For a longer beard, repeat Row 4.

Fasten off, leaving a long tail. Position the beard onto the face with the opening over the mouth. Sew into place with the yarn tail or matching embroidery floss. To make the beard furry and full, use a short-bristled brush or dog slicker brush to brush the beard in all directions.

ACCESSORIES AND MORE

Your doll is finished! There he or she is, a doll lovingly handcrafted from head to toe, by you. But is something missing? Does she need a prop? Is she never without her favorite handbag? Does he love his dog so much you can't picture him without it? Here's the part where you give your doll the little details that bring him or her to life.

I'll start with accessories that you'll add to your doll's body. These include glasses, a belt, a headband, jewelry, and a flower. There's a pattern for a tiny wrap. Next are hats. We'll see a baseball cap, a beanie, a fedora, and a cowboy hat. You'll then learn how to make a purse and a backpack. Crochet a little guitar for your doll. Animals are last. Choose a dog or a cat.

GLASSES WITH PLASTIC FRAMES

We'll be using stiffened felt, readily available at any craft store. It has structure enough to hold its shape, but you can also sew into it to attach it to your doll's head. Sunglasses can also be made using the felt option by gluing small pieces of tinted film on the back of the glasses.

Materials and Tools

■ STIFFENED CRAFT FELT IN THE COLOR OF YOUR CHOICE
■ SHARP CRAFT SCISSORS
■ TINTED FILM (OPTIONAL, FOR SUNGLASSES)
■ CRAFT GLUE (OPTIONAL, FOR SUNGLASSES)
■ MATCHING THREAD
■ SEWING NEEDLE

INSTRUCTIONS

Measure the doll's head from ear to ear across the front of the face. Take that measurement and add ¾"/2cm. Cut a large rectangle from the stiffened felt with the length you just calculated and width of 1"/2.5cm. Cut a notch in the very middle to create the center bridge that fits over the nose. Trim the sides to create the temples of the glasses (the arms that extend from the frame to the ears). You can now trim the individual rims of each eyepiece to create the look you want. Trim the top of the glasses as desired. Pierce the lens area with very sharp scissors and cut out the lens shape you want. Repeat for the other lens. If you're making sunglasses, cut small shapes from the film slightly larger than the openings, and using tiny dots of craft glue, attach the lenses behind the openings. Crease the edges of the frame to fit the face. Position the glasses in place and sew them to the tips of the temples just above the doll's ears, hiding the stitches in the hair, if desired.

GLASSES WITH WIRE FRAMES

Wire frames are made using craft wire, usually available in the jewelry section of the craft store. Although there are many different styles, the following pattern will give you a good basic shape to start with.

Materials and Tools

- WIRE CUTTERS
- 16- OR 20-GAUGE WIRE
- NEEDLE-NOSE PLIERS
- SEWING NEEDLE
- SILVER THREAD

INSTRUCTIONS

Cut a piece of wire the length of your doll's face ear to ear plus ¾"/2cm. With needle-nose pliers, bend the wire into shape, with right angles at the sides of the face. Bend each end into a tiny loop. Bend the center into the shape of the bridge of the glasses. Cut two smaller pieces of wire for the lenses. "Hook" the ends up over the main piece, crimping the ends to secure. Sew the glasses onto the face by sewing loops at each end above the ears with silver thread. Stitch the center over the bridge of the nose, if desired.

BELT AND HEADBAND

A simple strip of crocheted fabric can be used as a belt or a headband, and you decide how wide or narrow it should be.

Before you sew the pants to the doll, make a belt using surface-slip stitches. Using the worsted-weight yarn of your choice, make a slip knot, place it on your hook, and slip stitch around a stitch at the back of the pants one round below the waistline. Working sideways around the waist, slip stitch around each stitch. Fasten off and weave in ends. With metallic or colored embroidery floss and an embroidery needle, come up in the front just above the belt, then back down just under the belt, holding a loose loop to one side. Secure the loop with another tiny stitch, then make a larger straight stitch across the loop to complete the buckle. Knot the thread close to the surface and thread back into the pants.

For a belt that is separate and attached to the body, the process is a bit different. You'll crochet a long strip that is attached to your doll's waist with a few simple stitches.

This belt pattern may also be used for a headband.

Materials and Tools

■ WORSTED-WEIGHT OR SPORT-WEIGHT YARN IN THE BELT COLOR OF YOUR CHOICE (REFER TO PAGE 12 FOR A LIST OF RECOMMENDED YARNS) ④ OR ③
■ CROCHET HOOK: 3.5MM (SIZE E-4 U.S.)
■ YARN NEEDLE
■ EMBROIDERY FLOSS (OPTIONAL)
■ EMBROIDERY NEEDLE (OPTIONAL)
■ CRAFT GLUE (OPTIONAL)
■ FELT (OPTIONAL)

Stitches and Techniques Used

■ CHAIN (CH), PAGE 18
■ SINGLE CROCHET (SC), PAGE 19

INSTRUCTIONS

BELT:

Row 1: Ch 27, sc into 2nd ch from hook and each additional ch—26 sts.

Continue ch 1, turn, sc in each st across for additional rows for a wider belt.

Fasten off and wrap around doll. Use yarn tail to sew strip created into a ring and secure in place on the doll with a few stitches. Weave in ends.

FINISHING:

Add a buckle with straight stitches and embroidery floss, or embellish the belt with cut and glued felt pieces.

HEADBAND:

Start with a ch of 38 sts and then follow the Belt instructions, making the strip as thick or as narrow as you like. Attach it to your doll's head with a few tiny stitches.

JEWELRY

Some people are never without their favorite pair of earrings or a strand of pearls. Jewelry is easy to add and a cute little detail that won't go unnoticed.

LOOP earrings

Thread a yarn needle with yarn the color of your choice, knot the end, and insert the needle from the back through to the front of the ear. If desired, add a bead on the strand of yarn at this point. Make a loop at the base, wrap the yarn around the base and knot it, then stitch back down into the ear. Repeat for the other side.

Bead earrings

For simple stud earrings, thread an embroidery needle with a neutral color of floss, knot one end, and insert the needle from the back through to the front of the ear. Thread a bead or beads onto the floss and insert the needle back down into the ear, knotting it behind the ear and securing the bead. Hide the end by inserting the needle back into the ear and clipping the thread short, close to the surface.

OTHER earrings

Large metal jump rings also make great-looking hoop earrings (note that they are a bit more delicate). Simply open the jump ring with a set of needle-nose pliers, insert the open end into the ear lobe,

and turn. Close the jump ring with the pliers and twist so the opening is within the ear. You can also put beads or charms on the jump ring before closing it up for dangly earrings.

BRACELET/ NECKLACE

A bracelet and a necklace are both made the same way. Thread embroidery floss onto a needle and come up on the back of the wrist or neck. Thread beads onto your floss and wrap around the wrist or neck. Insert the needle back into the doll near the same point where you came up. Knot it tightly on the other side and weave it back into the doll. Clip the thread short, letting it retract back inside the doll. (Note that you can also do this with thick strands of embroidery thread in silver or gold. No beads required!)

FLOWER EMBELLISHMENT

Sometimes all an outfit or hairstyle needs is a little feminine touch. Add a cute tiny flower to a cardigan, stitch one onto a purse, or add one to a hat for a sweet detail. Varying weights of yarn will yield different sizes of flowers. Lighter weight yarn will make a smaller flower, while worsted or chunky yarn will make bigger ones. For a really tiny flower, try using crochet thread or embroidery floss.

Materials and Tools
■ YARN IN THE WEIGHT AND COLOR OF YOUR CHOICE
■ CROCHET HOOK: APPROPRIATE FOR CHOSEN YARN. HINT: MANY YARN LABELS SUGGEST A HOOK SIZE.
■ YARN NEEDLE

Stitches and Techniques Used
■ ADJUSTABLE RING, PAGE 20
■ CHAIN (CH), PAGE 18
■ SINGLE CROCHET (SC), PAGE 19
■ HALF DOUBLE CROCHET (HDC), PAGE 21
■ DOUBLE CROCHET (DC), PAGE 22
■ SLIP STITCH (SL ST), PAGE 19

INSTRUCTIONS
Rnd 1: Make an adjustable ring, ch 1, work 9 sc into the ring. Pull closed—9 sts.

Rnd 2: *Ch 1, (dc, hdc) into next st, sl st into next st; rep from * to end of rnd, working last sl st into first st of the rnd.

Fasten off, leaving a long tail.
Use tail and a yarn needle to sew into place.

WRAP

Whether it's used for a night out or just to keep a chill away, a tiny wrap around your doll's shoulders is a sweet accessory. It's crocheted in a soft sport-weight yarn for better drape. Make the wrap narrow by only crocheting a few rows, and you've made a tiny scarf!

Materials and Tools

■ SPORT-WEIGHT YARN IN THE COLOR OF YOUR CHOICE (REFER TO PAGE 12 FOR A LIST OF RECOMMENDED YARNS) (3)
■ CROCHET HOOK: 3.5MM (SIZE E-4 U.S.)
■ YARN NEEDLE

Stitches and Techniques Used

■ CHAIN (CH), PAGE 18
■ HALF DOUBLE CROCHET (HDC), PAGE 21

INSTRUCTIONS

Rnd 1: Ch 45, (hdc, ch 1, hdc) into 3rd ch from hook (V-st made), *sk next 2 ch, V-st in next ch; rep from * across—15 V-sts.

Rows 2–8: Ch 1, V-st into each ch-1 space across.

Fasten off and weave in ends.

BASEBALL CAP

A ball cap is probably the most popular kind of hat among men, and tons of women choose this sporty look, too. Whether to mask a bad-hair day or just to keep the sun out of the wearer's eyes, a baseball cap remains a casual favorite.

Materials and Tools

■ WORSTED-WEIGHT YARN IN THE COLOR(S) OF YOUR CHOICE (REFER TO PAGE 12 FOR A LIST OF RECOMMENDED YARNS) ④

■ CROCHET HOOK: 3.5MM (SIZE E-4 U.S.)

■ STITCH MARKER

■ YARN NEEDLE

■ EMBROIDERY FLOSS (OPTIONAL)

■ EMBROIDERY NEEDLE (OPTIONAL)

Stitches and Techniques Used

■ ADJUSTABLE RING, PAGE 20

■ CHAIN (CH), PAGE 18

■ SINGLE CROCHET (SC), PAGE 19

■ FRONT LOOPS ONLY (FLO), PAGE 28

■ SINGLE CROCHET TWO TOGETHER (SC2TOG), PAGE 24

INSTRUCTIONS
BASEBALL CAP:

Rnd 1: Make an adjustable ring, ch 1, work 6 sc into the ring. Pull closed—6 sts.

Rnd 2: Work 2 sc into each st around—12 sts.

Rnd 3: *2 sc into next st, sc into next st; rep from * to end of rnd—18 sts.

Rnd 4: *2 sc into next st, sc into next 2 sts; rep from * to end of rnd—24 sts.

Rnd 5: Sc into each st around.

Rnd 6: *2 sc into next st, sc into next 3 sts; rep from * to end of rnd—30 sts.

Rnd 7: *2 sc into next st, sc into next 4 sts; rep from * to end of rnd—36 sts.

Rnd 8: Sc into each st around.

BILL:

Change to second color for the bill of the cap, if desired.

Row 9: Ch 1, sc into FLO of last st of Rnd 8 and next 9 sts; leave remaining sts unworked—10 sts.

Rows 10–12: Ch 1, turn, working in both loops of each st, sc into each st across.

Row 13: Ch 1, turn, sc2tog, sc into next 2 sts, sc2tog, sc into next 2 sts, sc2tog—7 sts.

Row 14: Ch 1, turn, sc into each st across.

Rnd 15: Do not ch 1, do not turn, sc evenly spaced all the way around edge of hat; join with a sl st into first st of rnd. Fasten off and weave in ends.

CHILD'S BASEBALL CAP:

Rnd 1: Make an adjustable ring, ch 1, work 6 sc into the ring. Pull closed—6 sts.

Rnd 2: Work 2 sc into each st around—12 sts.

Rnd 3: *2 sc into next st, sc into next st; rep from * to end of rnd —18 sts.

Rnd 4: *2 sc into next st, sc into next 2 sts; rep from * to end of rnd—24 sts.

Rnds 5–8: Sc into each st around.

CHILD'S BILL:

Change to second color for the bill of the cap, if desired.

Row 9: Sl st next 9 sts; leave remaining sts unworked—9 sts.

Row 10: Ch 1, turn, sc into each sl st across—9 sts.

Row 11: Ch 1, turn, sc2tog twice, sc in next st, sc2tog twice—5 sts.

Rows 12 and 13: Ch 1, turn, sc into each st across.

Rnd 14: Do not ch 1, do not turn, sc evenly spaced all the way around edge of hat; join with a sl st into first st of rnd. Fasten off and weave in ends.

FINISHING:

To add a design to the front of the cap, use embroidery floss and a needle to stitch letters or a shape. Hide ends inside cap.

BEANIE

For male or female dolls, a beanie is an effortless style choice. Crochet it in stripes, changing color every other row, or make a solid color. Add a tie to the back to make a "do-rag."

Materials and Tools

- WORSTED-WEIGHT YARN IN THE COLOR(S) OF YOUR CHOICE (REFER TO PAGE 12 FOR A LIST OF RECOMMENDED YARNS) **4**
- CROCHET HOOK: 3.5MM (SIZE E-4 U.S.)
- STITCH MARKER
- YARN NEEDLE

Stitches and Techniques Used

- ADJUSTABLE RING, PAGE 20
- CHAIN (CH), PAGE 18
- SINGLE CROCHET (SC), PAGE 19
- HALF DOUBLE CROCHET (HDC), PAGE 21
- SLIP STITCH (SL ST), PAGE 19

INSTRUCTIONS

BEANIE:

Rnd 1: Make an adjustable ring, ch 1, work 6 sc into the ring. Pull closed—6 sts.

Rnd 2: Work 2 sc into each st around—12 sts.

Rnd 3: *2 sc into next st, sc into next st; rep from * to end of rnd— 18 sts.

Rnd 4: *2 sc into next st, sc into next 2 sts; rep from * to end of rnd—24 sts.

Rnd 5: Sc into each st around.

Rnd 6: *2 sc into next st, sc into next 3 sts; rep from * to end of rnd—30 sts.

Rnd 7: *2 sc into next st, sc into next 4 sts; rep from * to end of rnd—36 sts.

Rnds 8–13: Sc into each st around. Fasten off and weave in ends.

CHILD'S BEANIE:

Rnd 1: Make an adjustable ring, ch 1, work 6 sc into the ring. Pull closed—6 sts.

Rnd 2: Work 2 sc into each st around—12 sts.

Rnd 3: *2 sc into next st, sc into next st; rep from * to end of rnd —18 sts.

Rnd 4: *2 sc into next st, sc into next 2 sts; rep from * to end of rnd—24 sts.

Rnd 5–8: Sc into each st around. Fasten off and weave in ends.

BACK TIE (OPTIONAL):

Row 1: Ch 10, sc in 2nd ch from hook, sc in next ch, hdc in next ch, 2 hdc in next ch, sl st in next ch, 2 hdc in next ch, hdc in next ch, sc in next ch, sl st in last ch—11 sts.

Fasten off and leave a long tail for sewing. Weave long tail through to the middle of the tie, and sew to back of beanie, wrapping the yarn around the center to secure and to resemble a knot in the tie. Weave in ends.

FEDORA

Fedoras evoke a certain coolness. Men or women can wear them. Stylish in brown, black, or gray, they can also be made in a natural "straw" color with a black band for a Latin look.

Materials and Tools

■ WORSTED-WEIGHT YARN IN THE COLOR(S) OF YOUR CHOICE (REFER TO PAGE 12 FOR A LIST OF RECOMMENDED YARNS) ④

■ CROCHET HOOK: 3.5MM (SIZE E-4 U.S.)

■ STITCH MARKER

■ YARN NEEDLE

■ EMBROIDERY FLOSS (OPTIONAL)

■ EMBROIDERY NEEDLE (OPTIONAL)

Stitches and Techniques Used

■ ADJUSTABLE RING, PAGE 20

■ CHAIN (CH), PAGE 18

■ SINGLE CROCHET (SC), PAGE 19

■ FRONT LOOPS ONLY (FLO), PAGE 28

INSTRUCTIONS

FEDORA:

Rnd 1: Make an adjustable ring, ch 1, work 6 sc into the ring. Pull closed—6 sts.

Rnd 2: Work 2 sc into each st around—12 sts.

Rnd 3: *2 sc into next st, sc into next st; rep from * to end of rnd—18 sts.

Rnd 4: *2 sc into next st, sc into next 2 sts; rep from * to end of rnd—24 sts.

Rnd 5: *2 sc into next st, sc into next 3 sts; rep from * to end of rnd—30 sts.

Rnd 6: Sc into each st around.

Rnd 7: *2 sc into next st, sc into next 9 sts; rep from * to end of rnd—33 sts.

Rnd 8: Sc into each st around.

Rnd 9: *2 sc into next st, sc into next 10 sts; rep from * to end of rnd—36 sts.

Rnd 10: Sc into each st around.

To make a contrasting colored band, change color at the end of Rnd 10.

Rnd 11-13: Sc into each st around.

Change back to main color if you changed after Rnd 10.

BRIM:

Rnd 14: Working in FLO, *2 sc into next st, sc into next 5 sts); rep from * to end of rnd—42 sts.

Rnd 15: Sc into each st around.

Rnd 16: *2 sc into next st, sc into next 6 sts; rep from * to end of rnd—48 sts.

Rnd 17: Sc into each st around.

Rnd 18: *2 sc into next st, sc into next 7 sts; rep from * to end of rnd—54 sts.

Rnds 19-20: Sc into each st around.

Rnd 21: *2 sc into next st, sc into next 8 sts; rep from * to end of rnd–60 sts.

Rnd 22: Sc into each st around.

Rnd 23: *2 sc into next st, sc into next 9 sts; rep from * to end of rnd–66 sts.

Fasten off and weave in ends. Fold up the brim at Rnd 14, keeping the front pointed down. At the top of the hat, push the center inward and pinch the sides in to create the classic fedora shape. Secure with a few short stitches through all layers if desired.

CHILD'S FEDORA:

Rnd 1: Make an adjustable ring, ch 1, work 6 sc into the ring. Pull closed—6 sts.

Rnd 2: Work 2 sc into each st around—12 sts.

Rnd 3: *2 sc into next st, sc into next st; rep from * to end of rnd—18 sts.

Rnd 4: *2 sc into next st, sc into next 2 sts; rep from * to end of rnd—24 sts.

Rnds 5 and 6: Sc into each st around.

Rnd 7: *2 sc into next st, sc into next 7 sts; rep from * to end of rnd—27 sts.

Rnd 8: Sc into each st around.

Rnd 9: *2 sc into next st, sc into next 8 sts; rep from * to end of rnd—30 sts.

For a contrasting hat band, crochet Rnd 10 in a different color, and change back to hat color at the end of the round.

Rnd 10: Sc into each st around.

BRIM:

Rnd 11: Working in FLO, *2 sc into next st, sc into next 4 sts; rep from * to end of rnd—36 sts.

Rnd 12: *2 sc into next st, sc into next 5 sts; rep from * to end of rnd—42 sts.

Rnd 13: Sc into each st around.

Fasten off and weave in ends. Roll up Rnds 11–13 for the brim of the hat, keeping the front pointed down. At the top of the hat, push the center inward and pinch the sides in to create the classic fedora shape. Secure with a few short stitches through all layers if desired.

COWBOY HAT

Good news! Cowboy hats aren't just for cowboys anymore! Head out to any music festival and you'll see scads of cowboy hats on girls and guys. They beat the heat while adding a Western flair to any outfit. Yeehaw!

Materials and Tools

■ WORSTED-WEIGHT YARN IN THE COLOR(S) OF YOUR CHOICE (REFER TO PAGE 12 FOR A LIST OF RECOMMENDED YARNS) **(4)**

■ CROCHET HOOK: 3.5MM (SIZE E-4 U.S.)

■ STITCH MARKER

■ YARN NEEDLE

■ EMBROIDERY FLOSS (OPTIONAL)

■ EMBROIDERY NEEDLE (OPTIONAL)

Stitches and Techniques Used

■ ADJUSTABLE RING, PAGE 20

■ CHAIN (CH), PAGE 18

■ SINGLE CROCHET (SC), PAGE 19

■ FRONT LOOPS ONLY (FLO), PAGE 28

INSTRUCTIONS
COWBOY HAT:

Rnd 1: Ch 6, sc into 2nd ch from hook, sc into next 3 ch, 3 sc in last ch; rotate piece to work into bottom side of ch, sc in next 4 ch, 3 sc in starting ch (ch skipped at the beginning of the rnd)—14 sts.

Rnd 2: Sc in next 4 sts, 2 sc in next 3 sts, sc in next 4 sts, 2 sc in next 3 sts—20 sts.

Rnd 3: Sc in next 4 sts, 2 sc in next 6 sts, sc in next 4 sts, 2 sc in next 6 sts—32 sts.

Rnds 4–7: Sc into each st around.

Rnd 8: *2 sc into next st, sc into next 7 sts; rep from * to end of rnd—36 sts.

Rnds 9–11: Sc into each st around.

Rnd 12: *2 sc into next st, sc into next 8 sts; rep from * to end of rnd—40 sts.

BRIM:

Rnd 13: Working in FLO, *2 sc in next st, sc in next 3 sts; rep from * to end of rnd—50 sts.

Rnd 14: Working in both loops, * 2 sc in next st, sc in next 4 sts; rep from * to end of rnd—60 sts.

Rnd 15: *2 sc in next st, sc in next 14 sts; rep from * to end of rnd—64 sts.

Rnds 16 and 17: Sc into each st around.

Fasten off and weave in ends. Slightly roll up brim of hat on the sides. At the top of the hat, push the center inward and pinch the sides in to create the cowboy hat shape.

CHILD'S COWBOY HAT:

Rnd 1: Ch 5, sc into 2nd ch from hook, sc into next 2 ch, 3 sc in last ch; rotate piece to work into bottom side of ch, sc in next 3 ch, 3 sc in starting ch (ch skipped at the beginning of the rnd)—12 sts.

Rnd 2: Sc in next 3 sts, 2 sc in next 3 sts, sc in next 3 sts, 2 sc in next 3 sts—18 sts.

Rnd 3: Sc in next 5 sts, 2 sc in next 3 sts, sc in next 5 sts, 2 sc in next 3 sts, sc in next 2 sts—24 sts.

Rnds 4–7: Sc into each st around.

Rnd 8: *2 sc into next st, sc into next 7 sts; rep from * to end of rnd—27 sts.

Rnd 9: *2 sc in next st, sc into next 8 sts; rep from * to end of rnd—30 sts.

BRIM:

Rnd 10: Working in FLO, *2 sc in next st, sc in next 4 sts; rep from * to end of rnd—36 sts.

Rnd 11: *2 sc in next st, sc in next 5 sts; rep from * to end of rnd—42 sts.

Rnd 12: *2 sc into next st, sc into next 6 sts; rep from * to end of rnd—48 sts.

Rnds 13 and 14: Sc into each st around.

Fasten off and weave in ends. Slightly roll up brim of hat on the sides. At the top of the hat, push the center inward and pinch the sides in to create the cowboy hat shape.

HANDBAG

Crochet a handbag for your doll in a solid color with a matching strap, or have fun mixing colors for a designer look. Alternate colors every row for a stripe effect. Vary the strap length according to the kind of purse you want to make. A shorter strap will be carried by hand, while a longer strap can be worn over the shoulder or across the body.

Materials and Tools

■ WORSTED-WEIGHT YARN IN THE COLOR(S) OF YOUR CHOICE (REFER TO PAGE 12 FOR A LIST OF RECOMMENDED YARNS) **(4)**
■ CROCHET HOOK: 3.5MM (SIZE E-4 U.S.)
■ YARN NEEDLE

Stitches and Techniques Used

■ CHAIN (CH), PAGE 18
■ SINGLE CROCHET (SC), PAGE 19
■ HALF DOUBLE CROCHET (HDC), PAGE 21
■ HALF DOUBLE CROCHET TWO TOGETHER (HDC2TOG), PAGE 27
■ BACK LOOPS ONLY (BLO), PAGE 28
■ SINGLE CROCHET TWO TOGETHER (SC2TOG), PAGE 24

INSTRUCTIONS

HANDBAG:

Row 1: Ch 10, hdc into 3rd ch from hook and next 7 ch—8 sts.

Row 2: Ch 2 (does not count as a st here and throughout), turn, hdc into each st across.

Row 3: Ch 2, turn, 2 hdc into first st, hdc into next 6 sts, 2 hdc into last st—10 sts.

Rows 4–9: Ch 2, turn, hdc into each st across.

Row 10: Ch 2, turn, hdc2tog, hdc into next 6 sts, hdc2tog—8 sts.

Row 11: Ch 2, turn, hdc into each st across.

FLAP:

Row 12: Ch 1, turn, working in BLO, sc in each st across.

Row 13: Ch 1, turn, sc into each st across.

Row 14: Ch 1, turn, sc2tog, sc into next 4 sts, sc2tog—6 sts.

Row 15: Ch 1, turn, sc2tog, sc into next 4 sts, sc2tog—4 sts.

Fasten off and weave in ends. Fold purse in half so that Row 1 meets up with Row 11. Rows 12–15 form the flap.

Row 16: Join yarn with a sl st at bottom corner of back of handbag. Sl st through both layers of the purse up to the flap, then around the edge of the flap, and down through both layers to the opposite corner. Weave in ends.

STRAP:

Row 1: For a handbag, ch 17. For a shoulder bag, ch 27. Sc into 2nd ch from hook and each remaining ch across—16 sts (for handbag), 26 sts (for shoulder bag).

Row 2: Ch 1, turn, sc into each st across.

Fasten off and leave a long tail for sewing. Attach each end of the strap just inside the top opening of the bag at the seamed sides. Weave in ends.

BACKPACK

Typically, only ladies or little girls carry handbags, but most everyone has toted around a backpack at some point. They're comfortable, hands-free, carry loads of books, and can even be fashionable. Crochet one out of a solid color or alternate each row for stripes.

Materials and Tools

■ WORSTED-WEIGHT YARN IN THE COLOR(S) OF YOUR CHOICE (REFER TO PAGE 12 FOR A LIST OF RECOMMENDED YARNS) **(4)**

■ CROCHET HOOK: 3.5MM (SIZE E-4 U.S.)

■ YARN NEEDLE

Stitches and Techniques Used

■ CHAIN (CH), PAGE 18

■ SINGLE CROCHET (SC), PAGE 19

■ SINGLE CROCHET TWO TOGETHER (SC2TOG), PAGE 24

■ HALF DOUBLE CROCHET (HDC), PAGE 21

■ HALF DOUBLE CROCHET TWO TOGETHER (HDC2TOG), PAGE 27

■ BACK LOOPS ONLY (BLO), PAGE 28

■ FRONT LOOPS ONLY (FLO), PAGE 28

INSTRUCTIONS

BACKPACK:

Row 1: Ch 10, hdc into 3rd ch from hook and next 7 ch—8 sts.

Rows 2–4: Ch 2 (does not count as a st here and throughout), turn, hdc into each st across.

Row 5: Ch 2, turn, hdc into next 3 sts, 2 hdc into next st, hdc into next 4 sts—9 sts.

Row 6: Ch 2, turn, hdc into next 4 sts, 2 hdc into next st, hdc into next 4 sts—10 sts.

Row 7: Ch 2, turn, hdc into each st across.

Row 8: Ch 1, turn, sc into BLO of each st across.

Rows 9 and 10: Ch 1, turn, sc in each st across.

Row 11: Ch 2, turn, hdc into FLO of each st across.

Row 12: Ch 2, turn, hdc into each st across.

Row 13: Ch 2, turn, hdc into next 4 sts, hdc2tog, hdc into next 4 sts—9 sts.

Row 14: Ch 2, turn, hdc into next 3 sts, hdc2tog, hdc into next 4 sts—8 sts.

Rows 15–17: Ch 2, turn, hdc into each st across.

FLAP:

Rows 18–20: Ch 1, turn, sc into each st across.

Row 21: Ch 1, turn, sc2tog, sc into next 4 sts, sc2tog—6 sts.

Row 22: Ch 1, turn, sc2tog, sc into next 2 sts, sc2tog—4 sts.

Fasten off. Weave in ends. Fold piece in half so that Row 17 lines up with Row 1. Sew edges together down each side.

FLAP EDGING:

Join yarn with sc at beginning of flap edge, work 5 more sc evenly spaced to center of flap, ch 5 (for button looop), work 6 sc evenly spaced to end of flap. Fasten off and weave in ends. Sew a button to the front of the backpack at Row 3. Attach loop made in flap edging over button.

STRAP (MAKE 2):

Ch 16. Fasten off and sew each end to the back of the backpack, 3 sts apart at the top and 6 sts apart at the bottom.

Weave in ends.

ANIMAL COMPANIONS

When you think of a certain person, do you instantly think of her loyal canine companion? Is his cat the center of his universe? Here's where you'll create a pet for your doll. Choose a dog, and give him short or floppy ears. Make a cat and pick fluffy yarn or something smooth and silky. Each of these patterns will require yarn in the texture of your choice, embroidery floss, and safety eyes. Craft stores online carry a great variety of animal and cat safety eyes. Felt and a little dab of craft glue can be substituted for safety eyes if you'd prefer.

DOG

Make man's best friend with either worsted or bulky fuzzy yarn to match the look you're going for. Fur or eyelash yarn can be used to great effect to make a shaggy dog, but take care to trim areas of excess furriness so facial features will show (around eyes, etc.). Legs, tail, and muzzle should be made with matching worsted-weight yarn if using bulky or fur yarn for the head and body. The pattern is for a solid-colored animal but color changes within rows will make spots if you'd like.

Materials and Tools

■ WORSTED-WEIGHT OR BULKY YARN IN THE HEAD AND BODY COLOR OF YOUR CHOICE (A) (REFER TO PAGE 12 FOR A LIST OF RECOMMENDED YARNS) **(4)** OR **(5)**

■ WORSTED-WEIGHT YARN IN LEG, TAIL, MUZZLE, AND EAR COLOR OF YOUR CHOICE (B) (REFER TO PAGE 12 FOR A LIST OF RECOMMENDED YARNS) **(4)**

■ CROCHET HOOK: 3.5MM (SIZE E-4 U.S.)

■ STITCH MARKER

■ YARN NEEDLE

■ POLYESTER FIBERFILL STUFFING

■ BLACK EMBROIDERY FLOSS

■ EMBROIDERY NEEDLE

■ TWO 6MM OR 9MM SAFETY EYES IN THE COLOR OF YOUR CHOICE

■ SMALL ANIMAL NOSE (OPTIONAL)

Stitches and Techniques Used

■ ADJUSTABLE RING, PAGE 20
■ CHAIN (CH), PAGE 18
■ SINGLE CROCHET (SC), PAGE 19
■ SINGLE CROCHET TWO TOGETHER (SC2TOG), PAGE 24
■ SURFACE SINGLE CROCHET (SURFACE SC), PAGE 30

INSTRUCTIONS

BODY:

Rnd 1: Starting at head end (front) of body with A, make an adjustable ring, ch 1, work 6 sc into the ring. Pull closed—6 sts.

Rnd 2: Work 2 sc into each st around—12 sts.

Rnd 3: *2 sc into next st, sc into next 3 sts; rep from * to end of rnd—15 sts.

Rnds 4–8: Sc into each st around.

Rnd 9: *Sc2tog, sc into next 3 sts; rep from* to end of rnd—12 sts.

Insert stitch marker to hold your place. Stuff body firmly.

Rnd 10: Sc2tog around—6 sts.

Fasten off, leaving a 6"/15cm tail. Thread yarn needle with the tail and weave through stitches of last round. Pull tightly to close up the hole and insert yarn needle back into the head, pulling tail through and snipping close to surface of the fabric to hide end.

LEG (MAKE 4):

Rnd 1: Starting at paw end with B, make an adjustable ring, ch 1, work 6 sc into the ring. Pull closed—6 sts.

Rnds 2–6: Sc into each st around.

Rnd 7: Sc2tog, sc into next 4 sts —5 sts.

Stuff sparingly and sew to body, positioning two close together near the front of the body, and two on each side of the tail end of the body. With black embroidery floss, stitch toe separations onto each paw with 3 short straight stitches.

TAIL:

Rnd 1: Starting at tip of tail with B, make an adjustable ring, ch 1, work 4 sc into the ring. Pull closed—4 sts.

Rnd 2: Sc into each st around.

Repeat Rnd 2 until tail is desired length. Fasten off and leave a 9"/23cm tail. Sew to body.

HEAD:

Rnd 1: Starting at top of head with A, make an adjustable ring, ch 1, work 6 sc into the ring. Pull closed—6 sts.

Rnd 2: Work 2 sc into each st around—12 sts.

Rnd 3: *2 sc into next st, sc into next 3 sts; rep from * to end of rnd—15 sts.

Rnds 4 and 5: Sc into each st around.

Rnd 6: *Sc2tog, sc into next 3 sts; rep from * to end of rnd—12 sts.

Insert stitch marker to hold your place. Insert safety eyes between Rnds 4 and 5, 3 or 4 sts apart. Stuff head firmly.

Rnd 7: Sc2tog around—6 sts.

Fasten off, leaving a long tail (12"/30.5cm). Thread yarn needle with the tail and weave through stitches of last round. Pull tightly to close up the hole and insert yarn needle back into the head, coming back up next to one eye. Stitch twice in a diagonal across the top of the eye to create an eyelid (if using fuzzy or bulky yarn, stitch only once). Repeat for other side. Knot tail and hide within head.

MUZZLE:

Rnd 1: Starting at tip of nose with B, make an adjustable ring, ch 1, work 4 sc into the ring. Pull closed—4 sts.

Rnd 2: Work 2 sc into each st around—8 sts.

Rnd 3: *2 sc into next st, sc into next 2 sts; rep from * to end of rnd—12 sts.

For jowls on your dog's muzzle, continue with Row 4. For a muzzle without jowls, fasten off and leave a long tail for sewing. Follow instructions for assembly below.

Row 4: Turn muzzle piece and working in a diagonal toward the beginning ring, work 4 surface sc evenly spaced across rounds to center ring, sl st into center ring, turn, work

4 surface sc evenly spaced into back down to Rnd 3, about 4 stitches from the first stitch of Row 4. Sl st into Rnd 3 and fasten off, leaving a long tail for sewing.

Insert animal nose in the center of the muzzle, or with a scrap of yarn or embroidery floss, stitch the nose onto the muzzle with straight stitches. Sew muzzle to dog's head with yarn tail, stuffing as you go. Weave in ends.

Use Floppy Ear or Short Ear pattern.

FLOPPY EAR (MAKE 2):

Rnd 1: Starting at tip of ear with B, make an adjustable ring, ch 1, work 6 sc into the ring. Pull closed—6 sts.

Rnd 2: *2 sc into next st, sc into next st; rep from * to end of rnd—9 sts.

Rnds 3–6: Sc into each st around.

Rnd 7: Sc2tog, sc into each st around—8 sts.

Rnd 8: Sc into each st around.

Rnds 9 and 10: Sc2tog, sc into each st around—6 sts at the end of Rnd 10.

Fasten off and leave a long tail. Flatten ear and sew to top of head along Rnd 3.

SHORT EAR (MAKE 2):

Row 1: With B, ch 4, sc into 2nd ch from hook and next 2 ch—3 sts.

Row 2: Ch 1, turn, sc2tog, sc into next st—2 sts.

Row 3: Ch 1, turn, sc2tog—1 st.

Row 4: Ch 1, turn, sc into st.

Fasten off and leave a long tail for sewing to head. Weave tail down side of ear to Row 1. Sew ear to top of head at Row 3. Fold down Rows 3 and 4.

Sew head to body at a slight angle with matching yarn.

cat

Cat safety eyes really bring an amigurumi cat to life. I use fuzzy yarn and brush the surface to make cats. Fur or eyelash yarn can be used to make a long-haired cat, but take care to trim areas of excess furriness so facial features will show (around eyes, etc.). The legs and tail should be made with matching worsted-weight yarn if using fur yarn for the head and body. The pattern is for a solid-colored animal but variegated yarn will make your cat spotted.

Materials and Tools

- WORSTED-WEIGHT OR BULKY YARN IN THE COLOR OF YOUR CHOICE (A) (REFER TO PAGE 12 FOR A LIST OF RECOMMENDED YARNS) **4** OR **5**
- CROCHET HOOK: 3.5MM (SIZE E-4 U.S.)
- STITCH MARKER
- YARN NEEDLE
- POLYESTER FIBERFILL STUFFING
- BLACK OR WHITE EMBROIDERY FLOSS
- EMBROIDERY NEEDLE
- TWO 9MM SAFETY EYES IN THE COLOR OF YOUR CHOICE
- SMALL ANIMAL NOSE (OPTIONAL)

Stitches and Techniques Used

- ADJUSTABLE RING, PAGE 20
- CHAIN (CH), PAGE 18
- SINGLE CROCHET (SC), PAGE 19
- INVISIBLE DECREASE (INVDEC), PAGE 25

INSTRUCTIONS

BODY:

Rnd 1: Starting at head end of body, with A, make an adjustable ring, ch 1, work 6 sc into the ring. Pull closed—6 sts.

Rnd 2: Work 2 sc into each st around—12 sts.

Rnd 3: *2 sc into next st, sc into next 3 sts; rep from * to end of rnd—15 sts.

Rnds 4–9: Sc into each st around.

Rnd 10: *Sc2tog, sc into next 3 sts; rep from * to end of rnd—12 sts.

Insert stitch marker to hold your place. Stuff body firmly.

Rnd 11: Sc2tog around—6 sts.

Fasten off, leaving a 6"/15cm tail. Thread yarn needle with the tail and weave through stitches of last round. Pull tightly to close up the hole and

insert yarn needle back into the head, pulling tail through and snipping close to surface of the fabric to hide end.

TAIL:

Row 1: Ch 13, sc into 2nd ch from hook and next 11 ch—12 sts.

Fasten off and leave a 9"/23 cm tail. Sew to hind end of the body.

FRONT LEG (MAKE 2):

Rnd 1: Starting at paw end, make an adjustable ring, ch 1, work 5 sc into the ring. Pull closed—5 sts.

Rnds 2–7: Sc into each st around.

Rnd 8: Sc2tog, sc into next 3 sts—4 sts.

Stuff sparingly and sew to body, positioning close together near the front of the body. With black or white embroidery floss, stitch toe separations onto each paw with short straight stitches.

BACK LEG (MAKE 2):

Rnd 1: Starting at paw end, make an adjustable ring, ch 1, work 5 sc into the ring. Pull closed—5 sts.

Rnds 2–5: Sc into each st around.

Rnd 6: Sc2tog, sc into next 3 sts—4 sts.

Stuff sparingly and sew to body, positioning on either side of the tail end of the body. With black or white embroidery floss, stitch toe separations onto each paw with short straight stitches.

HEAD:

Rnd 1: Starting at top of head, make an adjustable ring, ch 1, work 6 sc into the ring. Pull closed—6 sts.

Rnd 2: Work 2 sc into each st around—12 sts.

Rnd 3: *2 sc into next st, sc into next 3 sts; rep from * to end of rnd—15 sts.

Rnds 4 and 5: Sc into each st around.

Rnd 6: *Invdec, sc into next 3 sts; rep from * to end of rnd—12 sts.

Insert stitch marker to hold your place. Insert safety eyes between Rnds 4 and 5, 4 sts apart. Insert nose between eyes, one round down. Stuff head firmly.

Rnd 7: Sc2tog around—6 sts.

Fasten off, leaving a long tail (12"/30.5cm). Thread yarn needle with the tail and weave through stitches of last round. Pull tightly to close up the hole and insert yarn needle back into the head, coming back up next to one eye. Use black or white embroidery floss to make whiskers. Thread needle with floss; do not knot the end. Insert the needle where you want the whiskers to be, come back up close to the same spot, and knot the floss. Trim to desired length. Repeat for as many whiskers as you'd like on each side.

EAR (MAKE 2):

Row 1: Ch 4, sc into 2nd ch from hook, (hdc, ch 2, hdc) into next ch, (sc, sl st) into last ch—6 sts.

Fasten off and leave a long tail for sewing to head. Sew ear to top of head at Row 3. Sew head to body at a slight angle with matching yarn.

RESOURCES

FLESH-TONE YARNS

Caron Simply Soft: color Lt. Country Peach #9737; worsted weight yarn (4)

Caron Simply Soft: color Sand #0006; worsted weight yarn (4)

Lion Brand Vanna's Choice: color Beige #123; worsted weight yarn (4)

Hobby Lobby I Love This Yarn: color Toasted Almond #150; worsted weight yarn (4)

Cascade 220: colors Beige #8021, Sienna #7821; worsted weight yarn (4)

Red Heart Super Saver: color Warm Brown #0036; worsted weight yarn (4)

OUTERWEAR/ SKIRT YARNS

Martha Stewart Crafts Extra Soft Wool Blend: color Gray Pearl #550; worsted weight yarn (4)

Kollage Riveting Sport Denim Yarn: color Night Denim #7903; sport weight yarn (2)

Hobby Lobby I Love This Yarn Sport Yarn: colors Brown #160, Red #40, White #10; DK weight yarn (3)

Lion Brand Vanna's Glamour: colors Platinum #150, Onyx #153, Ruby Red #113; sport weight yarn (2)

Loops and Threads Impeccable: color Navy #01110; worsted weight yarn (4)

Caron Simply Soft Light: color Capri #0007; DK weight yarn (3)

Patons Classic Wool: color Natural Marl #77010; worsted weight yarn (4)

Red Heart Soft: color White #4600; worsted weight yarn (4)

Red Heart Shimmer: color Hot Pink #1715; worsted weight yarn (4)

Cascade 220: color Black #8555; worsted weight yarn (4)

HAIR/FUR YARNS

Cascade Pacific: color Dijon #57; worsted weight yarn (4)

Red Heart Soft: colors Honey #9114, Black #4614; worsted weight yarn (4)

Bernat Satin Sport: color Black #03040; DK weight yarn (3)

Cascade 220 Heathers: colors Mocha Heather #9446, Japanese Heather #2435; worsted weight yarn (4)

Bernat Alpaca: color Tundra #93013; bulky weight yarn (5)

Lion Brand Silky Twist: colors Oatmeal #207, Java #208; super bulky weight yarn (6)

Lion Brand Woolease Thick and Quick: color Spice #135; super bulky weight yarn (6)

Red Heart Stitch Nation Bamboo Ewe: color Buttercup #5230; worsted weight yarn (4)

Martha Stewart Crafts Extra Soft Wool Blend: color Lemon Chiffon #557; worsted weight yarn (4)

Cascade 220 Sport: color Ginger #858; sport weight yarn (2)

OTHER YARNS

Cascade Luna: color Mango #742; worsted weight yarn **(4)**

Caron Simply Soft: color Black #9727; worsted weight yarn **(4)**

Lion Brand Hometown USA: color Pittsburgh Yellow #158; super bulky weight yarn **(6)**

Vickie Howell for Bernat Sheep(ish): color Yellow(ish) #12; worsted weight yarn **(4)**

Hobby Lobby Yarn Bee Boucle Traditions Double Boucle: color Black #125; worsted weight yarn **(4)**

Hobby Lobby Yarn Bee Boucle Traditions: color Black #125; worsted weight yarn **(4)**

Lion Brand Woolease: color Cocoa #129; worsted weight yarn **(4)**

Lion Brand Vanna's Choice: colors White #100, Aqua #102, Taupe #125, Cranberry #180, Tangerine Mist #306; worsted weight yarn **(4)**

Red Heart Soft: colors Toast #1882, Tangerine #4422; worsted weight yarn **(4)**

Lion Brand Woolease: color Fisherman #099; worsted weight yarn **(4)**

Lion Brand Vanna's Glamour: colors Diamond #100, Gold #171; sport weight yarn **(2)**

Caron Simply Soft Light: colors Bubble Gum #0012, Riviera #0008; DK weight yarn **(3)**

Bernat Softee Baby: color Baby Denim Marl #30300; DK weight yarn **(3)**

Hobby Lobby I Love This Yarn: colors Red #40, Yellow #330, White #10, Buttercup #340, Brown #160; worsted weight yarn **(4)**

Hobby Lobby I Love This Yarn Sport Yarn: color Sun Yellow #210; DK weight yarn **(3)**

Martha Stewart Crafts Extra Soft Wool Blend: color Winter Sky #507; worsted weight yarn **(4)**

Caron Simply Soft: colors Grey Heather #9742, Grape #9610, Lemon #0017; worsted weight yarn **(4)**

Red Heart Super Saver: colors Lavender #0358, Plum Pudding #0940; worsted weight yarn **(4)**

Vickie Howell for Bernat Sheep(ish): colors Grey(ish) #3, Turquoise(ish) #17, Camel(ish) #10; worsted weight yarn **(4)**

Cascade 220: color Regency #9426; worsted weight yarn **(4)**

Cascade Luna: color White #701; worsted weight yarn **(4)**

Cascade 220 Heathers: color Cherry #2426; worsted weight yarn **(4)**

RESURCES

HOOKS

Clover Soft-Touch Hooks

Lion Brand Pearl
Acrylic Hooks

Tulip Etimo Hooks

POLYESTER FIBERFILL

Fairfield Poly-fil 100%
Polyester

Supreme Fiberfill

WHERE TO BUY

Lion Brand Yarn Company
lionbrand.com
1-800-258-YARN

Red Heart Yarns
redheart.com
1-800-648-1479

Bernat Yarns
bernat.com
1-800-351-8356

Cascade Yarns
cascadeyarns.com

Patons Yarn
patonsyarns.com
1-800-351-8357

Joann Fabric and Craft Stores
joann.com
1-888-739-4120

Hobby Lobby
shop.hobbylobby.com
1-800-888-0321

Michaels
michaels.com
1-800-MICHAELS

A.C. Moore Arts and Crafts
acmoore.com
1-888-ACMOORE

Annie's Attic
anniesattic.com
1-800-582-6643

WEBS, America's Yarn Store
yarn.com
1-800-FOR-WEBS

Yarnmarket
yarnmarket.com
1-888-996-9276

Herrschners
herrschners.com
1-800-441-0838

Knitting-Warehouse
knitting-warehouse.com
1-831-728-2584

Mary Maxim
marymaxim.com
1-800-962-9504

Jimmy Beans Wool
jimmybeanswool.com
1-877-JBW-KNIT

ACKNOWLEDGMENTS

This book is dedicated to my sweet niece, Jane, an angel, who was the fastest learning crocheter I ever taught, even as a lefty! I will always be so proud to be your aunt.

Thanks go first to my editor, Thom O'Hearn, who saw the potential in my ideas and understood my vision. Thanks, Thom, for allowing me to go crazy with my designs and encouraging me (and my creativity) all the way. Your patience and perspective were greatly valued. Also, many thanks to the rest of the book team: Kristi Pfeffer, KJ Hay, Karen Levy, and Lynne Harty.

I have to thank my literary agent to the stars, Kate McKean, who held my hand through the proposal process and advised me every step of the way. I couldn't have started this process without your belief in me… and I still owe you a coffee.

To Stacy Klaus at The Knitting Nest in Austin, Texas, who saw my work and told me to get out there, thank you! Without your encouragement, I wouldn't have started teaching, or tried to get in magazines, and you've supported me every step of the way.

To my Facebook fans and Twitter followers, thank you for letting me bounce ideas off you, for the enthusiasm you've shown all along, and for giving me confidence in my abilities. Every "like" counts!

Thank you to the yarn companies that graciously donated products to use in my book. Your generosity and attention mean so much.

Last but certainly not least, I thank my family: My loving and understanding husband, Paul, who played dual mommy/daddy roles for months while I escaped to coffee shops to write and rewrite patterns, and picked up the slack when I had to work late nights to meet a deadline. I love you. My sweet boys, Luke, Jack, and Levi, thank you for being the inspiration for everything in this book! Thanks for letting mommy get her work done and waiting patiently to play on my computer or for a snack. I did it for you! To my sisters, Jennifer, Kendra, and Jessica, and my amazing in-laws, Patrick, Rebecca, and Amy, thank you for your excitement and encouragement, and for hours of babysitting. Thank you to my mom, Vicki Landrum, for your never-ending love and support and belief in what I was doing. Thank you for inspiring me to be creative and crafty and a good mom.

Photo by Kelley Denby Photography

ABOUT THE AUTHOR

Allison Hoffman has been designing amigurumi patterns since she learned how to crochet. Her work has been seen everywhere, from *The Martha Stewart Show* to *Conan*, as well as in art exhibits around the United States. She is frequently featured in both pop-culture and craft publications, such as *Crochet Today*, *Interweave Crochet*, BoingBoing.net, PerezHilton.com, and more. She blogs at CraftyisCool.com and designs patterns for several yarn companies. She teaches amigurumi classes in Austin, Texas, where she lives with her husband, three little boys, and two Labs.

INDEX